un journaling

Daily writing exercises that are
NOT introspective
NOT personal
NOT boring

Dawn DiPrince   Cheryl Miller Thurston

PRUFROCK PRESS INC.
WACO, TEXAS

Prufrock Press Inc.
P.O. Box 8813
Waco, TX 76714-8813
Phone: (800) 998-2208
Fax: (800) 240-0333
http://www.prufrock.com

Table of Contents

Introduction

Writing can be an intimidating process for many people, no matter what their age. It can be revealing—too revealing. Some people just don't want to share intimate details about their thoughts, feelings and lives—at least not with others in a class or group. They may not have the level of trust necessary, and quite possibly for very good reason. Or they may not have the confidence necessary. Or they may simply be very private people.

Writing does not have to be a psychological journey. All the daily writing exercises in *Unjournaling* are entirely impersonal, while still challenging a writer's creativity and ingenuity. The exercises take writers out of themselves and involve them in playing with words, inventing characters, imagining and writing about situations involving others, and much more.

Most of all, *Unjournaling* encourages students of all ages to have fun with language. When students write frequently, and about many different topics, they become more comfortable with writing. Some of the writing prompts may seem silly, but we've learned that silly writing really helps writers loosen up. Their sentences become more fluid. They are less likely to freeze. Topics like those included in *Unjournaling* help ease the way for hesitant writers, while challenging the creativity of more experienced writers.

Unjournaling includes 200 writing prompts that are suitable for writers of all ages, from middle school through adult. We have tried to make them flexible and varied, as well as challenging and interesting. Teachers can use *Unjournaling* in the classroom, or individuals can use it on their own.

Sample responses to all of the questions are included in the last part of the book—a helpful tool for teachers or anyone who gets stuck completing an exercise and wants to see that it *can* be done. Reading what others have done can also open a writer's mind to different approaches and ideas he or she may not have considered. (The sample answers were written by a variety of people of all ages.)

Whether you are a teacher using the book in the classroom or an individual using it on your own, we hope you will enjoy *Unjournaling!*

Dawn DiPrince and Cheryl Miller Thurston

un journaling

Writing Prompts

1. Write a paragraph about a girl named Dot, but use no letters with dots (i, j).

2. *Silly* is a middle-aged man who combs his remaining limp strands of hair into an elabo-rate swirl over his bald spot, gluing them in place with hair spray and hoping no one will notice.

Silly is a golden retriever who slinks sheepishly off the sofa whenever his owner comes home, hoping—despite the piles of hair all over the cush-ion—that she won't notice he's been sleeping there.

What else is *silly*? Give three more examples.

3. Write a paragraph that includes at least 10 words that rhyme with *be*.

4. Write a paragraph about a cat attacking something, but don't use the words *hiss*, *scratch* or *pounce*.

5. Describe the gunky stuff that gets caught in the basket at the bottom of the sink. Don't use the words *disgusting* or *gross*.

6. A bad dude in a cowboy hat is walking into the saloon in a bad Western movie. He's looking dangerous and mad. Tell what happens, creating a happy ending.

7.
Write a paragraph that includes twenty words with double vowels. Examples: *poodle, peep, needle.*

8. How many ways can you find to say no? Write ten sentences that say no in various ways, but without using the word no.

9. When you write, it is important to fit your tone to your purpose. If you want the manager of Widget World to allow a return, even though the 30-day return period has passed, it's not a good idea to start your letter in this hostile tone: "I don't know what knucklehead came up with your policy, but I think it's stupid."

If you want to apply for a job as a manager of Widget World, it's not a good idea to start your cover letter in this casual tone: "Hey. I hear you need a Widget wonk, and I'm cool with that."

If you want to propose marriage to the manager of Widget World, it's probably not a good idea to start your letter in this formal tone: "Dear Ms. Applespot: After a careful analysis, I find that a legal partnership, i.e. marriage, between the two of us would be beneficial to both parties involved."

To match tone to purpose, use words that fit the circumstances. Imagine you are the manager of Widget World. You have been hoping for a raise, since you know you've done an excellent job. However, the owner of the store isn't exactly the sharpest tack in the drawer, in your opinion, and probably hasn't even noticed. Write a letter to the owner, choosing your tone carefully as you point out why you should have that raise.

10. Create a sentence with words that begin with the letters in *sentence*, in order. In other words, the first word in the sentence should begin with *s*, the second with *e*, the third with *n*, etc.

11. In one paragraph, describe a scene from any sport. Use these words somewhere in the paragraph:

bounced, struggled, spied, roared, collapsed, giggled (yes, *giggled!*).

12. Describe someone who looks bored. Don't use any form of the words *yawned* or *stared* or *sighed*.

13. Write one sentence consisting entirely of three-syllable words (not counting the articles *a*, *an*, and *the*).

14.
Write a sentence that makes sense reading either from left to right or right to left.

Example:

Bob liked Mary and Bill. Bill and Mary liked Bob.

See how long you can make the sentence.

15. As the writer for a clothing catalog, you must describe a sweater that is brown, beige, red-orange and purple. Describe the sweater, but use new, two-word descriptions for each color. (Catalogs rarely describe something as *black*, for example. They are more likely to say *ebony ink* or *midnight oil*.)

16.

Writers can often tell something about a character by what the character says and how he says it.

For example, if a third grader walks into a classroom and says, with a little bow, "Good afternoon, Mr. Fendlehessey. I am extremely pleased to be attending your class today, and I wish you a successful and satisfying lesson," the reader knows that student is probably not your average, ordinary American child—at least not from this century.

Try your hand at telling something about a character through his words, and how he says them. Imagine each of the characters below and write out what each might say in turning down an offer to go on a fishing trip.

- A teenaged boy turns down his grandfather.
- A businessman eager for a promotion turns down his boss.
- A wife just back from her weekly trip to the spa for a styling and manicure turns down her husband.

Unjournaling © Prufrock Press Inc.

17. Create a much more interesting version of this sentence:

The dog barked.

What kind of dog was it? Where was it? Why was it barking? How would you describe the barking? Make the sentence as interesting as possible by choosing your words and details carefully.

18. Here's what the artist called her painting:

Polar Bear Eating Vanilla Ice Cream in a Blizzard

To viewers, it looked like a plain white piece of canvas.

How might the artist describe what looks like a plain black canvas?

How about a plain blue canvas?

19. Like looking for a needle in a haystack is a descriptive phrase that we have all heard. Create five different descriptive phrases that mean the same thing.

20.

Here's a bit of a story, told in two and three-word sentences and phrases:

Bob cried. Elizabeth laughed. Sarah wondered why.

She asked. Elizabeth told her. "Bob lost."

"Lost what?"

"The bet."

"How much?"

"100 dollars"

"Ouch. He's crying. I see why."

Tell another bit of a story, using only two and three-word sentences and phrases.

21. Here's the last part of a newspaper story:

Neighbors called police when they noticed the pink gooey substance oozing from all the doors and windows of the modest ranch home.

Now write the first part of the story. Remember that a newspaper story starts right out answering the questions, "Who?," "What?," "Where?," "When?," "Why?," and "How?"

22. Brent told a joke. All five people in the room thought it was funny, though each one reacted differently. Describe the reactions of all five people.

23. Mr. and Ms. Pinehurst-Granola believe that school cheers are too violent. They don't like cheers like these:

*Hit 'em again.
Hit 'em again.
Harder! Harder!*

or

*Orange and black.
Sharks! Attack!*

To please the Pinehurst-Granolas, write a nice, gentle cheer for the Sharks.

24.

*What advice would a
DOG
give about life, if it
could talk?
Write that advice.*

25. What are the best reasons for doing nothing? List them.

26. Create an impression of a person, real or imaginary, by describing only the person's hands. Use only three sentences.

27. You are a writer who has a secret arrangement with the automobile industry. You will be paid $10.00 for every word you publish that includes the word *car*. (Examples: *scar cart, carp, carton*.) The hope is that repetition of the letters *c-a-r* will encourage people, subliminally, to want to buy cars.

You are starting a short story for a magazine. Write your first paragraph. How much money can you make using *c-a-r* in just that paragraph?

28. Many products today come with warnings that seem pretty obvious—and ridiculous. A hair dryer warning reads, "Do not use in tub." The carton for an iron says, "Do not iron clothes on your body." A jar of peanuts includes this note: "Warning: May contain peanuts." A chain saw box warning reads, "Do not attempt to stop chain saw with your hands."

Write five original and obvious warnings for anything you choose.

29. What kind of cartoon show might appeal to the over-age-65 audience? Imagine the show. Then, in 100 words or less, describe the show and its main character.

30. Write a paragraph in which each word begins with a letter of the alphabet, in order backwards, from Z to A. (The first word will begin with Z, the second with Y, the next with X, etc.) You may use the articles *a*, *an*, and *the* wherever you wish.

31.

Write a three-sentence paragraph about a *dog*, using no letters of the alphabet that appear before "m."

---

32. The general gives short, straightforward orders. His wife gives longer, chattier suggestions. How does the general tell his son to get up and mow the lawn? How does his wife tell him? Write out the words of each.

33. There is smoke. Where is it coming from? You investigate and are surprised by what you find. Describe what you discover.

34. Write an "un-ad" that tells the absolute truth about a product.

35. A friend has a blind date. You know the date. The person is not the most attractive person in the world but is very nice. Describe the person to your friend in a way that makes the person sound appealing. Be truthful, but don't use the word "nice."

36. Some people can't smell. In one paragraph, make them understand "skunk."

Unjournaling © Prufrock Press Inc.

37. *"When am I going to win the lottery?" asked Jenna.*

"When pigs fly," said Aaron. Keeping the same meaning, write five different, more original responses for Aaron.

40. Chris walks into the room. By describing only the reactions of the others in the room, let us know something about him.

38.

Yankee Doodle went to town,
A-riding on a pony.
Stuck a feather in his cap
And called it "macaroni."

Why on earth would Yankee Doodle call his feather "macaroni"? Write a plausible explanation.

---

39. Write three different sentences, each using the word *crumpled.* Create an entirely different image with each sentence.

41. A child finds an extraterrestrial in her backyard. It's not E.T. Who is it? What is it like? What does the child do? What happens? Explain.

42. Take the words of a popular love song and alter them so that the song is no longer about love. For example, you might change the beginning of "I Will Always Love You" to "I Will Always Hate You." Or you might start a new version of "I Want to Hold Your Hand" with "I Want to Hold My Nose." Change the lyrics of the entire song.

43. Describe a car, using at least five comparisons to food. (Use color as a comparison no more than once.)

44.

In one sentence, communicate

"fear."

45.

A mother wants to be as positive as possible with her toddler. Here's what she needs to communicate:

- *We should not bonk other toddlers on the head with our Tonka truck.*

- *We should not throw Mommy's new shoes in the toilet.*

- *We should not draw elephants on the living room wall with crayons.*

How can she tell her child not to do these things, but in a positive way?

46. Write a sentence in which the first word is one letter long, the second word is two letters long, the third word is three letters long, etc. See how long you can make the sentence.

47. *Why? Why? Why?* A four-year-old wants to know *why* chairs have four legs. You explain that it is for balance. "Why else?" she asks. She won't stop asking "*Why?*" until you help her think of every reason imaginable.

List all the reasons you come up with, both serious and fanciful.

48. King Kong *stomped* along the street. He *crushed* cars with his toes. He *ripped* people from their cars. In five sentences, what else did he do? Use descriptive verbs.

49. You can use 25 words—no more—for a billboard advertising a new product called *Zebra Wink.* Sell your product with those 25 words.

50.
Whine.
Bellyache.
Complain.
Moan.
Criticize.

Create a conversation that uses some form of each of these words.

51.

Write an incredibly awesome paragraph about your absolute favorite actor, singer or celebrity, using the most outstanding, excellent hyperbole in the whole, entire universe.

Hyperbole is extravagant exaggeration.

52.

Pick one of these subjects:

*cheerios, dishwashing liquid,
a computer mouse, a clothes dryer,
a bicycle tire.*

Write the subject at the top of a piece of paper.

Now write absolutely everything you can think of about this subject. Everything. No matter how mundane or boring or stupid it sounds, write down everything you can think of.

53.

Look at what you wrote for #52. Think some more. Keep writing!

Remember, you're going to say absolutely anything you can think of that's even remotely related to this subject.

54.

Look over all you have written about the subject you picked in #52. Undoubtedly, much of what you have written is rather dull. What is *most* interesting, though? What surprises you? What strikes you as funny?

Pull out something from what you have written, and use it as the basis of either...

• *a fake news story*

or

• *an anecdote to share with relatives or friends.*

55.

Write down 10 clichés or phrases that you hear often. (She's as *cute as a button*. He's as *strong as an ox*. It was *pretty as a picture*.)

Show that you are as smart as a whip by writing a paragraph that includes as many of these clichés as possible.

56.

Now rewrite the paragraph you just wrote (#55), eliminating the clichés and substituting fresh descriptions.

57. What is a *ditz*? How does a person act *ditzy*? Describe the meaning to an immigrant from *Lower Katzangorbia* who has been learning English from a book and doesn't understand slang.

58. You are a very, very sensible guy. You don't believe in exaggeration or pretty, flowery language. You think romantic stuff is for sissies.

Write a letter proposing to the woman you love and want to marry.

59. People often say, *"If we can send a man to the moon, surely we can figure out how to…"* Complete the sentence five different ways.

60. Write a *rhyme* paragraph. Each sentence must begin and end with words that rhyme with each other.

An example:

Spring is a wonderful *thing*. *Flowers* start to sprout with the help of rain *showers*.

61. Take a line from a favorite song and a line from a favorite movie. Incorporate both quotes into a paragraph.

For example, you might combine the lines, "Somewhere over the rainbow," and "Make my day" and write, "I've looked everywhere for my favorite red sweater. I've looked in my closet, in my dresser, even under the furniture. I wonder where it could be? Perhaps it's *somewhere over the rainbow*. If you can help me find it, you will really *make my day*!"

62.
"Oh, please, don't sneeze!"
Write a paragraph that includes as many words as possible that rhyme with *sneeze*.

63. Tell a fish story. Use as many *fishy* words as possible without actually writing about fish.

Examples of fishy words and phrases:

scales
whale of a good time
shrimp
clam up
net

64. Write about yesterday morning from the perspective of an everyday object or item—a salt shaker, a swing set, or a license plate, for example.

65. Write a *blue* paragraph, incorporating as many words that rhyme with the word *blue* as you possibly can.

66.

Poor Miss Shackleford has six-year-old Andrew Dunkle in her first grade class. In only three days, Andrew has caused Miss Shackleford to seriously consider resigning and becoming a waitress or a Chuck E. Cheese manager.

Miss Shackleford tries hard to see the good in every child and in every situation. She doesn't really believe that little Andrew has the potential to become an ax murderer, despite what he did to the goldfish.

Help Miss Shackleford write a letter to Mr. and Mrs. Dunkle, accentuating the positive but letting them know that Andrew needs to learn just a tad more self-discipline.

67. Pen a paragraph that is permeated with *p*s. In other words, write a paragraph that uses at least ten alliterative phrases that repeat the *p* sound.

Alliteration is the repetition of consonant sounds. Example:

Bob boiled beans with a bunch of broccoli and bits of bacon.

68.
Write a paragraph about *winter*, starting every sentence with the letter *W*.

69. Write a five-sentence paragraph of five-letter words (not counting *a*, *an*, or *the*.) Make the subject of your paragraph an animal.

70. List ten words that use *ph* to make an *f* sound. (Example: *phrase*.)

Then use all ten words in a paragraph.

71.
Update the story of Cinderella.

These days, Cinderella wouldn't be sweeping cinders. What would she be doing?

She wouldn't be riding in a carriage drawn by horses. What would she be riding in?

Retell the story for very modern children in very modern times.

---

72. Write a paragraph with at least nine words that start with the letter *a* and include nine letters.

73. Write a paragraph that starts with this sentence:

The grass smells red.

74. Use a thesaurus to look up synonyms for the word *crazy*. Then write a paragraph incorporating as many of the synonyms as possible. (Yes, you may refer to relatives—though perhaps fictional ones would be best!)

75. Most people believe *vomit* is an ugly word. Write a paragraph that incorporates at least 10 words *you* believe are ugly.

76. Write a conversation between two people, making the conversation consist entirely of questions.

Example:

"Do you want to grab a hamburger?" asked Chris.

"Do I look like someone who would ever let beef pass her lips?" asked Amber.

See how long you can make the conversation.

77. "Yipes," said the zebra. "I've lost my stripes." Continue the paragraph, using as many words as you possibly can that rhyme with *yipes*.

79.

Write a paragraph about a toddler eating her first piece of birthday cake—but without using these words:

sticky, gooey, messy.

80. Burp! Slosh! Snort! Write a paragraph incorporating at least ten onomatopoetic words.

Onomatopoetic words are words that sound like what they mean. Examples:

beep
boing
swoosh
hiccup
plop
fizz

78. Write a paragraph about *Thanksgiving* that does not use the letter *t*.

81.

Rewrite "Mary Had a Little Lamb" so that
Mary has a new animal, and she's taking it somewhere other
than to school. In case you need a reminder of the words,
here they are:

Mary had a little lamb,
Little lamb, little lamb.
Mary had a little lamb.
Its fleece was white as snow.

Everywhere that Mary went,
Mary went, Mary went.
Everywhere that Mary went,
The lamb was sure to go.

It followed her to school one day,
School one day, school one day.
It followed her to school one day,
Which was against the rules.

It made the children laugh and play,
Laugh and play, laugh and play.
It made the children laugh and play
To see a lamb at school.

82. Bippity-boppity-boo! Create your own fairy godmother. What does she look like? What does she have to offer you? Explain how she helps you. Describe her personality.

85. Finish this sentence three different ways, creating a different feeling with each sentence:

As Antonio opened the door, he gasped to see . . .

83.

Write a three-sentence paragraph about the view out an apartment window, without using the word "the."

84. Write 10 food and people similes. In other words, compare a person (real or imagined) to food. For example, you might say, "Franco is as assertive as a wilted piece of lettuce," or, "Marianna's hair is as red as tomato soup." Your comparisons should create a very clear image of the person.

86. Write a three-sentence paragraph using only the first half of the alphabet, letters *a-l*. (You may not use *t, m, s* or any other letter that appears past *l* in the alphabet.)

87. Describe something bland in one sentence that really makes a reader feel how bland it is.

88. There are only three words in the English dictionary that start with *dw*:

dwell

dwindle

dwarf

Write a paragraph that incorporates all three of these *dw* words. (If you want, throw in some slang *dw* words, like *dweeb*. Or invent a few new *dw* words to add to your paragraph.)

89. Austin's mother sings too much. She sings while doing laundry. She sings while making dinner. She sings while driving to work. Worst of all, she sings when she is driving Austin and his friends to their soccer games or to the mall.

Describe a typical car ride with Austin, his friends, and his mother. What is his mother singing? How does she sound? What is Austin doing? What are his friends doing? Create a picture of the scene, in words.

90.
Some ideas are just bad ideas. Using a hair dryer in the bathtub is a bad idea. Buying a pet mouse when you already have a pet boa constrictor is a bad idea. Washing your red shirt with your white underwear is a bad idea. Using your hand to unclog a running garbage disposal is a bad idea.

List 10 more extremely bad ideas.

91.

The answer is, "No."
What is the question?

The answer is, "Yes."
What is the question?

The answer is, "Maybe."
What is the question?

The answer is, "What
is the question?"
What is the question?

92. "Oops," muttered Miss
Klinkfelder.
    Why the "Oops"?
Describe what led up to Miss
Klinkfelder's "Oops."

93. Fatima is a very spoiled teen-
age girl. Show that she is
spoiled, without saying she is
spoiled, by describing what
happens when she doesn't get
a car for her birthday.

94. *"You're pulling my
leg!"* is an expression that
has nothing to do with real
legs. Write an explana-
tion that describes how the
expression originated. (Since,
of course, you probably have
no idea, your explanation will
be pulling the leg of anyone
who reads it!)

95. Write about an argument.
Make each sentence start with
the last letter of the previous
sentence. (If the first sentence
ends in an *e*, the next sentence should start with an *e*.)

96. What's *icky?* Write five sentences describing five *icky* things.

97.

Have you ever had a leg cramp? If so, you are in luck. There are countless cures for leg cramps. Here are just some of the "cures" many believe will stop a leg cramp:

- *Eat a teaspoon of yellow mustard.*
- *Lick salt off your hand.*
- *Pinch the skin between your nose and your mouth.*
- *Sleep with a bar of soap in your bed.*

While these certainly sound crazy, many people believe them. Invent a crazy sounding cure for leg cramps, hiccups, mosquito bites or warts. Write a paragraph convincing people that this cure is "crazy but true." You may want to include "quotes" from a person or doctor who has used your cure. You may want to include a so-called "scientific" explanation for why your cure works.

---

98. Only the best is good enough for Bartholomew. (Never call him Bart!) Describe a typical evening for him.

99. What if the sky were not blue, but red? List five effects this would have on everyday life.

100.

Sylvia McDaniel is still reeling from the breakup with her most recent boyfriend, who was what she liked to call *adjective impaired*.

He was always choosing the wrong adjectives. He called her hair *frizzy*, while she would have preferred *wavy*. He called her *bony*, while she would have preferred *slim*. He called her family *weird*, while she would have preferred *eccentric*.

He also described her beloved dog like this:

> *That squat little mutt has a stupid haircut. It is fat. It has stumpy legs. It is yappy, fussy, ill-behaved, and annoying.*

Rewrite his description of the dog as it might sound if he were *not* adjective impaired.

101.

Unbeknownst to most people, the chicken had *a lot* of reasons for crossing the road. What were at least five of them?

102. The young woman her friends call the *Queen of Cute* has a new puppy, and she's pampering it. How does the *Queen of Cute* describe her new little darling?

103. You know what an *orfinbellydorper* is. Most people don't. Explain to them what to do with one.

104.

Alissa's writing teacher says she is too wordy. Below is what she wrote for her last assignment, which was to describe a situation that caused someone to cry.

Help Alissa by rewriting the description and getting rid of the wordiness. Keep only what really helps tell her story:

Brittany, who was wearing a pink T-shirt, a pair of low-slung jeans that showed off her belly-button ring, and spiky heeled boots, set her casserole down on the table. It was the first casserole she had ever made, and she was proud of it.

She had followed the classic recipe on the can of green beans carefully, stirring in the cream of mushroom soup and topping the casserole with French-fried onion rings. She couldn't resist eating a couple of the onion rings, but most were now safely on top of the casserole. She nestled her green bean casserole in between the vegetarian lasagna and the lime and pineapple Jell-O salad and other homemade dishes at the potluck dinner.

She was so proud she felt like putting a little sign with her name on it in front of the dish. She imagined an elegant little place card with calligraphy, saying, "Green Bean Casserole Lovingly Prepared by Brittany." She resisted, though. However, she did grab a chair close

Unjournaling © Prufrock Press Inc.

to the buffet table so that she could watch what people put on their plates and keep an eye on the ones who took her casserole. She wanted to keep an eye on them and watch them smile.

She settled into a black beanbag chair. (She thought it was appropriate for a green bean casserole maker to sit in a beanbag chair.) Although she listened to Jessica chatter on and on about the cute guy in the backyard by the red cedar picnic table, she only half listened. She didn't even pay much attention to the cute guy, although he was very cute and just her type. She liked tall, dark-haired guys who were on the slender side and smiled a lot. This guy was definitely smiling a lot.

Suddenly she saw someone put a scoop of the casserole on his sturdy, disposable plate. She didn't know how he'd managed to get inside without her noticing, but it was the cute, dark-haired guy. Her innocent face lit up. A cute guy was going to be the first to taste the casserole! She watched him closely because she wanted to see where he would sit.

But just as the guy put the green bean casserole on his plate, he said loudly, "What is this??? My plate is ruined! Who the heck doesn't know that you are supposed to drain the green-bean water out of the green beans before you put them in a casserole!!! Look at this mess!!!"

Jessica jumped up to give him another plate as Brittany burst into tears. She slipped from the room and went into the bathroom with the yellow flowered wallpaper. She sobbed and sobbed. Her first attempt at cooking had been a failure.

105. Write a very, very, very long question, with a very, very, very short couplet for an answer. (A couplet is simply two lines that rhyme.)

Example:

What did Mr. Elwin say when his wife locked him out of the house for coming home late when he was supposed to stay home that night and take her out to dinner for their anniversary, which he forgot?

*Move over,
Rover.*

106. Write another very, very, very long question with a very, very, very short couplet for an answer.

107. Complete the following ten different ways: *"Never . . ."*

108.

*Jack and Jill went up the hill
To fetch a pail of water.
Jack fell down and broke his crown,
And Jill came tumbling after.*

There is too much left out of this story. Who were Jack and Jill? How did they go up that hill? Did they walk? Ride a horse? Drive in a car? Why did they need a pail of water? Why didn't they just turn on a faucet? What made Jack fall down? How far did he fall? How serious was his "crown" injury? What made Jill tumble? Was she hurt?

Rewrite the story, filling in details to tell us what really happened.

109. Oddly enough, many *unk* words suggest something unpleasant. Write an unpleasant paragraph using the words *drunk, dunk, junk, skunk, stunk,* and *gunk.*

110. You are a farmer who wants personalized license plates. You aren't allowed to use more than seven letters and one hyphen or space. Come up with at least three ideas for your plates.

111. List three tactful but true things a person might say about Aunt Krissie's awful beet juice and lima bean Jell-O salad.

112. Shoot the moon. Write a story that includes 20 "oo" words.

113. Olivia has been criticized by her boyfriend for not expressing her feelings enough. "I never know what you think about anything!" he says. "You never give me any details. You shut me out of your thoughts and your life!"

Olivia decides to teach him a lesson. When he comes to pick her up one night, she shares, completely, every detail and thought in her head from the time they leave the house until they get in the car and shut the door. What does she say?

114.
Write four sentences made up of four four-letter words each.

115. Different groups often use slang that others don't understand. A teenaged skateboarder may use slang that is baffling to his parents. A grandparent may use slang that sounds silly to her grandchildren. The kitchen staff in a café may use slang that a soccer mom wouldn't understand. Computer geeks use slang that only other computer geeks understand.

Write a paragraph about a movie or a concert, using as much slang as possible. (You choose the kind of slang.) Be sure to overdo it!

116. Everyone in the group knew better than to say, "How are you?" to Mildred. Once again, though, someone forgot.

Write down Mildred's lengthy response.

117.
Here's what William hopes:

He sincerely hopes that, with time and patience and firm but gentle guidance and love, his daughter Angelica, who has insisted upon being called "Cobra Girl" ever since she got the tattoo down the left side of her neck, will have someone besides the police escort her home sometimes. He hoped she might start volunteering at the nursing home again and maybe even get a job, using that high school diploma of hers for something besides a liner in her sock drawer.

Tell what Cobra Girl has in mind.

118.

Write a four-line song or poem about *mayonnaise*.

119. It was a great truck, a fantastic truck, the truck of Carter's dreams. No one had ever seen a truck like it. It made Carter so happy.

Describe his truck.

120. In writing, show that a room has a very, very bad smell—but without saying it has a very, very bad smell.

121. Your life may depend on it. You're a spy. You're in danger. You have to get off an island, fast. You have arranged a signal with the owner of a boat. If he receives a note inviting him to a party, but without using the letter *a*, he knows to come for you, fast. To avoid suspicion if the note is intercepted, you want to be sure and include all the details about the party, including the reason for it.

Write your note. Be careful, though. One accidental *a* means you won't be rescued!

122.

You are paying $10.00 per word to advertise in the classified section of the Upscale Times, a newspaper for a very wealthy area of town. You want to offer your services as a dog sitter.

Write a convincing ad, but don't spend more than $200.00.

123.

Everyone hates it when Uncle Milhouse tells a story. It's not that his stories are bad—or at least they wouldn't be if he would just stick to the story. The problem is, he wanders. He'll say something like:

> Back in 1972, you wouldn't believe the tornado that hit our town. That was the year my dad got laid off at the factory…the pickle factory, it was. They were called Fickle Pickles, and they were the best darn dills you ever ate. Well, maybe my grandma's were just a tad better, to tell you the truth. She said her secret was to add a little cinnamon to the jars. Now, my wife, your Aunt Letitia, she says that's nonsense, that you can't add cinnamon to pickles, but, well, Grandma insisted that's what she did. Grandma was kind of known for her odd ideas. She could have put cinnamon in her pickles. I know for a fact that she put vinegar in her cherry pies, and they sure were good. It was probably because the cherries were fresh. She picked them straight off the tree in her backyard—the tree that got knocked over when a truck landed on it in 1972. It was during that gosh-awful tornado we had, and that truck, it just…

You get the idea. How does Uncle Milhouse tell the story of what happened when his sister tried to elope with a used car salesman?

124. Kaitlyn's mommy has a tendency to overuse the word *awesome*. If Kaitlyn drinks her milk, her mother says, "*Awesome!*" If her dad asks Kaitlyn to hand him the remote control, and she does, her mother says, "*Awesome!*" If Kaitlyn puts one tiny blue dot on a piece of paper and says, "It's a tree, Mommy!" her mother says, "*Awesome!*" Kaitlyn and her mother are going to the supermarket this morning. Write a paragraph describing their trip to the store, incorporating Kaitlyn's mommy's favorite word.

125. Write a paragraph on a subject of your choice, using only one-syllable words.

126. Here's the beginning of a paragraph:

Quenton felt queasy after eating quince and quail.

Finish the paragraph, using as many *qu* words as possible. Try for at least 10.

127.

Mac is a person who loves himself. He loves himself very, very, very much.

Show how much Mac thinks of himself by describing some of his actions, in one paragraph. Describe only his actions, not his thoughts.

128. Mr. and Mrs. Alfredo Wilkowitz named their son **Hokey Pokey Wilkowitz.** Not surprisingly, Hokey wants to know what they were thinking. Explain for them, clearly but kindly.

129. The answer is *mouthwash.* What is the question? Write five possible questions for that answer. (Try for originality—something more than, "What can I use to freshen my breath?")

130. Newspaper writers are supposed to be concise and stick to the facts. Marcella Romano has been criticized for being too concise. For example, she turned in this story last week:

There was a fight yesterday on Main Street at 1:00 a.m. It was a bad one.

Fill in the details for Marcella.

131.

Write a paragraph that starts with this sentence:

Why can't we just get some tattoos or something?

End your paragraph with this sentence:

The ring maker will be here in 10 minutes.

132. Penelope wants to close her restaurant. It is very successful, but she has to work long, long hours, and she is tired.

Her husband, however, doesn't want her to close it. He likes all the money it brings in, and he can be very cranky and hard to live with when he doesn't get his way.

Penelope decides the answer is to *cause* her business to be less successful, so that she will eventually have to close it. She starts by replacing three popular items on the menu each week with three dreadful entreés.

To help her out, name three new menu items for her, and write a short description of each. Remember, it's important to Penelope that her restaurant *fails*.

133.

Write an original tongue twister.

Some ideas:

- Use a lot of words that start with and/or include the same letter, as in *Peter Piper Picked a Peck of Pickled Peppers.*

- Or use a lot of words that are very similar to each other, like *group* and *goop* or *spot* and *slot*.

134. Write a sentence with every single word beginning with either *a* or *t*.

135. In one sentence, describe something (not someone) that is *very ugly*. Create a vividly ugly image, with words.

136.

Write a letter to an animal, creating a very clear mood with the tone of your letter. Are you going to address your dog? The neighbor's dog? A fish at the dentist's office? A lobster in a tank at a seafood restaurant? A penguin at the zoo? Think about why you are writing to this animal—to save it from being a fur coat, to threaten a lawsuit if he doesn't stop his constant barking during "Survivor"? Are you going to be serious? Silly? Whimsical? Funny? Or…?

137. The prisoner stood before the court and said, "Mistakes were made," and "I'm sorry for what happened."

"The way he puts it, you'd hardly guess that he had anything to do with that burglary," muttered the woman whose store he broke into.

Rewrite the prisoner's words, to more accurately reflect what really happened.

138.

Here's your chance to break the rules. See how many adjectives you can use in a paragraph to tell us as little as possible about a person walking into a party and catching everyone's eye. Choose vague adjectives that don't really help create a picture. (Adjectives, to refresh your memory, are words that describe nouns. Examples of boring adjectives: a *nice* boy, a *good* time, a *happy* baby.)

139. Now do the opposite of what you just did in item #138. Take the same paragraph and replace the boring adjectives with more interesting adjectives. Examples: *agitated* alligator, *slimy* bowl of soup, *stone-aged* computer with a *pea-sized* hard drive.

Unjournaling © Prufrock Press Inc.

140.

"The letter was sent" is a passive sentence.
"Hank sent the letter" is an active sentence.

"The game was won by us" is passive.
"We won the game" is active.

"I am loved" is passive.
"Alfred loves me" is active.

Active sentences have someone performing the action in the sentence, instead of receiving it. They are almost always much stronger than passive sentences.

Try your hand at improving the following passive description of a car accident. Rewrite it so that all the sentences are active.

> *The semi truck was plowed into by a PT Cruiser that was driven by a middle-aged former hippie who is still sad about having to give up his Volkswagen bus. The PT Cruiser was ruined by the impact. The former hippie was taken to the hospital by an ambulance. The ambulance was driven by a show-off taking his first turn at driving. The ambulance was driven too fast by him, and it was hit by a Porsche when a red light was ignored by both him and the Porsche driver—a cute little thing whose father had allowed her to take it for a short spin. All the wrecks were survived by all the people involved.*

141. Add one sentence that completely changes the impression this description makes:

The new teacher sitting at her desk slowly looked up at the class. She cleared her throat carefully several times and then, in a voice so soft the students could barely hear her, said, "Excuse me. Excuse me." Students giggled a bit and kept right on talking.

142. Great-grandpa Rotondo doesn't understand what a video game is. Or an iPod. Or text messaging.

Pick one of the above— or any other technological invention or process that wasn't around when Great-grandpa was younger. Explain what it is in terms that even the most un-technological person can understand.

143. The letters *tion* are very common at the end of English nouns. Here are just a few:

station, nation, anticipation, flirtation, vacation, combination, expectation, centralization, regurgitation.

Write a four-line poem in which each line ends in a *tion* word. (If you're on a roll, go ahead and make the poem longer than four lines.)

144. Somebody's sitting behind you on the bus. You hear only one side of an odd cell phone conversation, but it is intriguing and alarms you.

What do you hear?

Unjournaling © Prufrock Press Inc.

145. What would blue taste like

if you could chew it?

. . . .

146.

Abraham Lincoln's famous first sentence from the Gettysburg Address is "Fourscore and seven years ago our fathers brought forth on this continent, a new nation, conceived in liberty and dedicated to the proposition that all men are created equal." Copy the form of the sentence as much as possible, but update the subject matter to note a wedding, a birth, or some other "event."

For example, instead of saying "Fourscore and seven years ago," You might begin your sentence with "Two years and seven months ago..."

Try three different updates.

147. What if the shape *round* did not exist, except as the shape of the earth and moon?

Looking at just your immediate world, how would your life be different?

148. Write a sentence (or more than one sentence) about celebrating a holiday. Use exactly 100 letters—no more, no less.

149.

Create a *super hero* that the world needs. Your super hero must be entirely original, unlike any super hero you know of who has ever been created before.

Is the hero male or female? What special powers does he/she have? What problem will he/she solve for the world, or for a certain population of the world? Will the hero solve a really important problem, or just a smaller, annoying problem?

150.
Use all five vowels (a,e,i,o,u) at least once in a sentence about *gravy.*

151. Madison is so *happy*. In one paragraph, show that she is happy, but don't use the word *happy* or even a synonym for *happy*.

152. Write a sentence with no "ascenders" or "descenders." Ascenders or descenders are letters that have parts that extend above or below the main part of the letter in most type fonts: *b, d, f, g, h, i, j, k, l, p, q, t, y.* (Capital letters don't count.)

153. Here are the letters you can use:

e, s, a, t, r, c, n, m, h, w, d.

How many sentences can you write, using only these letters?

154. Write a short conversation that might take place between two people who are unlikely ever to meet. For example, you might have Brad Pitt talk to Benjamin Franklin or Hillary Clinton talk to King Tut. You might write a conversation between your third grade teacher and Orlando Bloom, or Martha Stewart and the crazy guy at the end of your street who seems to be collecting old tires.

155.

Jasmine wrote an e-mail to her best friend Erin, telling all about the *stupid* thing her boss did that day. Just as she finished, the phone rang. As she picked up the phone, she accidentally hit "Eric" instead of "Erin" in her address book. Eric is her boss.

Jasmine decided never ever to go to work again.

What on earth did she write? (Note: She did not swear.)

156. How many different ways can you say that precipitation fell—without actually using the words *"Precipitation fell"*?

157. Write a fake news story that includes the following words:

tater tot casserole
zipper
geraniums
karate.

158.

Three people are stuck in an elevator:

- a teenager with green hair and many body piercings
- a pastry chef
- a church organist.

Write the conversation they have as they wait.

---

159. Write a paragraph consisting of only *six letter words* (not counting *a*, *an*, or *the*).

160. You have undoubtedly heard the children's song, "Here We Go 'Round the Mulberry Bush." Explain why they might be going around a mulberry bush.

161.

"I request some money." Rewrite this sentence as each of the people listed below might word it. For each person, set the scene with one sentence. Then tell what the person said.

- A teenager to a parent.
- A bank robber to a teller.
- A woman to her ex-husband.
- A couple to a loan officer at a bank.
- A policeman to a driver.
- A dissatisfied customer to a store owner.
- A man who walked into a glass door to the concierge.

162. **Write a short essay or story that includes 26 sentences.** The first sentence must begin with the letter A, the second sentence with B, the third with C and so on, until you have used the entire alphabet.

163. "I wouldn't marry you even if you were the last man on earth," said Nadine.

Jeremy just smiled. He thought she was kidding.

She wasn't.

Help Nadine get through to Jeremy by completing the following sentence five different ways:

*I
wouldn't
marry
you
if…*

164. Write a three-sentence paragraph with every word beginning with the letter *s* (except for the articles *a, an,* and *the*).

165.

They say opposites attract. Use at least five pairs of opposites in a paragraph about some kind of transportation.

Examples:

*weak/strong
loud/quiet
high/low.*

166. A person's choice of a dog is said to express something about his or her personality. Choose five individuals whose names are well-known nationally. What kind of dog would you choose for each? Why? Explain.

167. Write a paragraph that starts with a *one-word sentence*, followed by a *two-word sentence*, then a *three-word sentence*, then a *four-word sentence*, etc.

How far can you go? Can you get as high as ten sentences?

168. Eldora Fishbein is about to become a grandparent. She doesn't want to be called *Grandma* or *Nana* or *Granny* or any traditional kind of grandmotherly name. She doesn't want to be called by her first name, and she doesn't want to be called *Mrs. Fishbein.*

Come up with five name ideas for her, and tell why they might be appropriate.

169.

Write a paragraph describing a place to eat. Use every letter of the alphabet at least once.

170.

Carlos is a poet. Write a message for his answering machine that reflects his personality.

171. As this is being written, a show called "What Not to Wear" is popular on the cable channel TLC. Imagine more possible shows on a "what *not* to do" theme. Describe at least one idea. (Don't forget to give the show a name.)

172. Write a paragraph that starts and ends with the word *computer*.

173.

The Bulwer-Lytton Fiction Contest is held every year to recognize the author of the worst possible opening line for a book. (Find more information at www.bulwer-lytton.com, where www stands for "Wretched Writers Welcome.") To enter, contestants simply submit the worst sentence they can imagine to begin a book.

The contest is in "honor" of Edward George Bulwer-Lytton, who began a book in 1830 with this long sentence: *It was a dark and stormy night; the rain fell in torrents—except at occasional intervals, when it was checked by a violent gust of wind which swept up the streets (for it is in London that our scene lies), rattling along the housetops, and fiercely agitating the scanty flame of the lamps that struggled against the darkness."*

Try your hand at writing a really bad sentence for the contest.

174.

Describe someone who is making a fashion statement, whatever that statement might be.

175.

Who makes you laugh? Why? Do your best to explain what makes the person funny.

176. Give ten useful pieces of advice to a specific person or group, beginning each piece of advice with *"Always…"* For example, you might consider advice to your child or your future child, advice to a parent, advice to a teacher, or advice to the President of the United States.

177. You've heard this expression:

Woe is me.

Address a different situation:

Woe is Joe.

Write Joe's melodramatic description of his woes. (Or write *Jo*'s melodramatic description of *her* woes.)

178. Why does it snow? Why do we have earthquakes? Why do leaves turn brown? Write a farfetched explanation of any natural phenomenon. For example, you could explain how rain is a result of the sun sweating because of the excessive heat.

179.

Write a paragraph that shows a stereotypical character doing something stereotypical. Examples:

A *ditzy blonde is trying on shoes at the mall.*

A *quiet, mousy librarian wearing glasses is putting away books.*

Then go back and change one sentence so that your character is no longer stereotypical—and much more interesting to the reader.

180.
Write a news paragraph that includes the following words:

cantaloupe, tooth-paste, guitar, flashlight, flip-flops.

181. *Invent new words.*
Choose a six-letter word. Add a letter to invent a new, original word. Define this word.

Now, change one letter in your new word to create another new word. Define this word.

Use the original word and both of the new words in a paragraph.

182. Prepositions are those little words that we don't pay much attention to but use all the time. Just a few examples:

of, into, at, by, to, up, on, by, in.

Write a paragraph about the final moments of a tied basketball game *or* someone's encounter with a used car salesman at a dealership—*without* using any of the prepositions just mentioned.

183. Choose a name randomly from the phone book. (Make sure it is someone you don't know.) Create a character based on the sound of this name. Reveal something about the character by describing him or her going into a restaurant for dinner.

184. You can tell a lot about a person by what he or she says. Here are some things Grandma Dorothy always says:

"You can never be too dressed up."

"A woman should never ask a man to dance."

"He is quite a snappy dresser."

Based on these sentences, imagine what kind of person Grandma Dorothy is. Write a paragraph describing her. Feel free to use any or all of her quotations.

185. You've heard song parodies such as *On Top of Spaghetti* (to the tune of "On Top of Old Smoky"). Perhaps you have listened to Weird Al Yankovich's parodies like *Lasagna* (to the tune of "La Bamba"). Or perhaps you have heard the singing group Capitol Steps, which performs parodies like *God Bless My SUV* (To the tune of "God Bless the USA").

Write your own parody of a well-known song, either an old standard or something more recent.

186.

For five years, *Webster's New International Dictionary* included an entry for the word *dord*. However, *dord* is not an actual word. (Even dictionary makers can make mistakes!) Invent your own definition for the word.

Write a paragraph using your newly defined word.

187.

Dictionary Diving. Open your dictionary and select a word that a person would not normally use in conversation. Include that word in a paragraph. (If you are feeling really brave, dictionary dive five times and select five unusual words to incorporate into one paragraph.)

188.

Choose a fictional or real-life character. How would he or she react in a crisis?

Imagine that your character's car has broken down in a dangerous area of the city. Write a description of your character's reaction.

189.

In English, writers generally use *ah-choo* to describe the sound made by a sneeze. In Russian, the sound is *ap-chi*. In Chinese it is *han-chee*. In Czech-oslovakian, it is *kychnuti*. Create five more ways to describe the sound a sneeze makes.

Then use them all in a paragraph about someone with allergies.

190. Imagine you are the newest employee of Rumors, Inc., and your sole job is to write clever hoax e-mail stories that people will believe. Write a story that is just crazy enough to be true—one that would be believable to the millions of people who forward crazy-sounding e-mail stories.

Here are a few sample ideas:

- Beware of crooks using boxes of corn flakes to steal your identity.

- Dog lovers, beware. Cats can cause some breeds of dogs to commit suicide.

- Guard your earlobes! Outbreaks of earlobe theft have been reported in all major U.S. cities over the past six months.

191.

Place this sentence in a paragraph where it will make sense:

Bea had never before wanted to be a bee.

192. Some say you can tell a lot about a person by the vehicle he or she drives. **Picture a car.** (Or is it a truck? Or an SUV?)

In your mind, rummage through this car. Check it out from every angle.

Describe the car and the man or woman who goes with it.

193.

The *Jar Jar Binks* character in *Star Wars: Episode I* was intended to be endearing and serve as comic relief. Instead, audiences have found *Jar Jar* to be rather annoying. What if you could write the annoying *Jar Jar* out of the Star Wars prequels? Write the beginning of a missing chapter that gets rid of *Jar Jar*.

194.

Euphemisms are polite words for something unpleasant. For example, we often say *passed on* instead of *died* or *kicked the bucket.*

New neighbors have just moved in, and they are asking who lives in the house on the corner. It's Arnold, the weirdest guy in the neighborhood. Describe Arnold to them, being truthful, but using euphemisms to describe his bizarre behavior.

195.

Allegorical names generally give a hint about who a character is. *Herman Pocketprotector* might be a nerd, for example, or *Hazel Scuttlebutt* a busybody.

Invent two characters with allegorical names. Then write a conversation between them. What they say should reflect the personality suggested by their names.

196.

Write a paragraph that starts with this sentence:

Why don't you learn how to talk to a rooster?

and ends with this one:

She slugged him.

197. Create a character named *Pat.* Who is Pat? You are creating him or her, so you decide.

How old is Pat? Who does Pat live with? What disappoints Pat? What recently made Pat unhappy? How unhappy? What does Pat like to do on Sunday afternoons?

Using what you know about Pat so far, describe Pat's meeting with *someone else* about *something, somewhere.*

198. How many ways can you find to communicate, in writing, *"He has a strong body"*—without actually writing, *"He has a strong body"*?

199. Songs for little children sometimes leave a lot to be desired. For example, *Rock-a-Bye Baby* has a baby falling out of a tree. *Little Bunny Foo Foo* has a bunny picking up mice and "boppin' 'em on the head."

Write a more cheerful and wholesome song for children, using the tunes of the above mentioned songs or creating your own tune.

200.
Describe the personality of a group that has a personality. It can be a real group or an imaginary group.

Is it a club? A team? A clique? A class at a school? The people who hang out at a certain restaurant or coffee shop? What kind of personality does the group have?

answer keys

NOTE: A number of people of varying ages were the guinea pigs for *Unjournaling*, trying out all the writing prompts and helping the authors refine the questions. The sample answers, below, are taken from the work of these very patient individuals.

Because many of the prompts in *Unjournaling* are not easy to complete, and because they often make unusual demands, students (and sometimes teachers!) may occasionally find themselves stumped as to possible answers. The answers below are included to help people over the hump when they are stuck and to provide samples of how *others* may approach each exercise. The samples are in no way meant to be models of what "ought" to be.

Dawn DiPrince and Cheryl Miller Thurston

1. Dot loved where she grew up, on the farm. She could never see herself as an urban dweller. She loved to be among the flowers, vegetables, cows and horses. Her mother encouraged her to go to school to become a nurse because Dot loved to help people, but Dot couldn't see herself anywhere else but on the farm.

2. **Silly** is a little old lady and her poodle, wearing matching sweaters and matching frizzy white hair-dos.

    Silly is a chocolate frosting-faced five-year-old who denies sneaking a chocolate cupcake.

    Silly is a ten-year-old with an attitude and a pack of Marlboros, thinking he looks so cool that others are looking at him with envy.

3. My Buddhist friend **Brea** and I **agree** that it is important to save small creatures from danger when need be. It is not uncommon to **see** us in our living rooms catching a **flea** or a **bee** and taking it outside. Brea even climbed up a **tree** so that **she** could see a little bug she had set **free**. We often **plea** with others to be as kind as **we** are. **Gee**, that would please **me**!

4. My ornery cat Snooker likes to tease and torment my sweet cat Marigold. He swats at her when she walks by and then lunges at her when she growls at him. He hunches down on all fours, does a little wiggle and then leaps up in the air and plops down right on top of her. It looks and sounds like two baby cougars vying for the role of alpha feline.

5. My worst chore is cleaning the little wad of unidentifiable food particles out of the kitchen sink drain. The gunk reminds me of rotting vegetables and old hamburger grease all mixed together. To get it out, you have to reach in and try to grab it, but it's slimy and it oozes out between your fingers. It smells bad, too—kind of like liver and okra casserole. I wouldn't be at all surprised to see cleaning the sink basket show up on an episode of *Fear Factor* someday.

6. A cowboy in a ten-gallon hat comes blasting through the saloon doors with a look on his face that says he would like to flatten someone. The bartender bravely says, "Howdy. What

can I get you?"

"Give me a strong drink," says the cowboy. "I just got fired."

"You must be upset," says the bartender, pouring the drink.

"I'm upset about getting fired, but I'm not upset about not being a cowboy anymore. I never wanted to be a cowboy in the first place."

"Really?"

"No. People take one look at me and think I'm a tough guy. I'm not. Inside I'm really a kind, sensitive guy."

"You could have fooled me," says the bartender, looking at the scar down the cowboy's face and his calloused hands. "What would you like to do instead?"

"What I'd really like to do is become a bartender."

The bartender stares at him in amazement and says, "You're kidding! All I ever wanted to do was be a cowboy!"

The cowboy trades his ten-gallon hat for an apron and starts washing glasses. The bartender walks out with a smile on his face, in search of a horse.

7. In the deep, dark woods, we never know what may be leaping or creeping through the weeds. It's best to keep our hoods on tight as we scoot through the underbrush in our boots. If we hear an owl hoot, we need to heed the warning and speed home quickly, taking care not to fall and make ourselves bleed. However, we should not brood over our fright. Instead, we should sit by a brook and feed ourselves some loopy noodles, for soon we will be back in the city, listening to motor scooters and horns tooting.

8. • "When you-know-what freezes over," said Jim's mother after he asked her when he could adopt a boa constrictor.
   • When the measure came up for a vote, the representative said, "Nay."
   • "Over my dead body!" yelled Samantha, after Edward asked for his ring back.
   • "Entry forbidden to anyone under 21," said the sign on the club door, making it apparent to the sixteen-year-olds that they weren't going to be partying there.
   • When Max asked his dad if he could borrow his BMW for prom night, the answer was a simple, "Dream on, sonny."
   • After a tree slammed through a window and smashed her television, Teresa's insurance claim came back stamped "Denied."
   • When David asked his boss if he would get a raise this year, she said, "Negative."
   • Shelby asked if she could get an extension on the assignment, but her teacher said it was "so unlikely as to be impossible."
   • When the candidate asked if I would vote for him, I politely said, "I believe I'd rather not."
   • Lily asked Benjamin out on a date, but he replied, cruelly, "Not if you were the last girl on earth."

9. Dear Mr. Sharp:

   Thank you for the opportunity to manage Widget World. I have enjoyed this position for over three years and would like to point out some of the wonderful things happening at Widget World under my supervision. In doing so, I think you will agree that a raise is a very appropriate way to reward such diligence.

I implemented the "No Tardy, You Party" incentive program. In short, the program rewards individual employees with an hour off Friday afternoon (paid) for every 90 consecutive days that they are on time. As a group, if all employees are on time for 90 consecutive days, they will all receive a catered lunch. Employees have responded to the program with great enthusiasm and have successfully and consistently reached their group goals for over a year now. Although the program has some costs involved, it is less than half the price we were paying in terms of lost worker productivity due to tardiness.

Last month, I had extra security lights and cameras added to the parking lot. Customers and employees commented that they feel safer and are very thankful for the concern we showed for their safety.

In an attempt to boost sales, I initiated the redesign of our logo. Since you adopted the updated logo, our brand recognition has improved and more customers than ever before have visited the Widget World store, resulting in a 20% increase in business in just the last three months. I welcome the opportunity to talk with you in person about the aforementioned accomplishments and trust that you will find a raise for me is in order. Please let me know if you have any questions, and thank you for your time.

Sincerely,
Holly Holder

10. S: Sick
    E: elephants
    N: never
    T: try
    E: energetic,
    N: nimble
    C: cartwheels,
    E: ever.

11. The tiny gymnast **bounced** up onto the balance beam and performed an incredible routine while the spectators **roared** their approval. When her score was posted, she **collapsed** into the arms of her coach, who gave her a big bear hug. Then she **spied** her mom and dad creating quite a ruckus on the sideline and she **giggled** uncontrollably. She **struggled** to regain her composure when she saw the TV cameras aimed at her, but she didn't succeed.

12. As the teacher droned on about statistics and pie charts, Ernie's eyes glazed over and his head started to droop. His teacher spoke sharply, and Ernie blinked his eyes, shook his head and took a deep breath. How he wished he were in English class where he could be doing goofy but interesting writing assignments. He started counting the tiles in the floor, just so he wouldn't fall asleep.

13. Melanie finally exercised intensely following Saturday's basketball tournament.

14.　　　Belatedly, Eric and Emily invited Audrey and Joseph and dancers and singers and bikers and skateboarders.

　　　Skateboarders and bikers and singers and dancers and Joseph and Audrey invited Emily and Eric, belatedly.

15. This striped version of our classic crew neck sweater is sure to spice up your winter wardrobe with bands of burned cinnamon mixed with citrus-fire twist. And as if that weren't enough—a subtle lavender musk takes its turn with a tailored tan to make this sweater a must-have.

16.　　　Teenaged boy: Yo, Gramps. Dude, fishing would be so cool, but Mom said I, like, have to clean my room today or she'll, like, ground me forever. Bummer!

　　　Businessman: Mr. Seal, that's the day I'm attending a seminar on techniques for increasing profits. I'd love to go fishing, but the company comes first. As a retired businessman yourself, I'm sure you understand.

　　　Wife: Fishing? Have you lost your mind? Look at my nails. Do you really think I'd like to dip my hands into a bucket of worms and spear those grimy little things onto hooks? Can you even imagine me doing such a thing, ever, let alone after I've just had Rose Temptation perfectly applied on all ten fingers?

17. The constant yap-yap-yapping of the peek-a-poo puppy on the porch next door was making Alfred wish with all his heart that he did not work from a home office.

18. Black canvas: Panther Stalking a Bat at Midnight in a Cave
Blue canvas: Floating Blueberries Lost at Sea

19. • Like looking for a sugar crystal in a sack of flour.
　• Like looking for an eyelash in the ocean.
　• Like trying to find a marshmallow dropped in a snow drift.
　• Like hunting for a blonde hair in a field of wheat.
　• Like trying to find a flea in a barrel of pepper.

20. Jenna jumped. So did Karen. Sam came over. Sam is four.
Jenna jumped faster. So did Karen. Sam jumped, too.
Jenna said something. Karen added something. Sam ran away.
Jenna laughed.
"Works every time."
"Like a charm."

21. There was confusion and chaos Tuesday morning in the Blueberry East subdivision. Eyewitnesses claim that a block-wide area was flooded with gallons of a pink substance, said to be liquid bubblegum.

　　　According to eyewitnesses, Al Conway, who resides at 427 East Magnolia, brought home a big barrel labeled "Contents Under Pressure" over the long holiday weekend. When neighbors asked him what it was, Conway said, "My kids chew bubblegum like it's going out of style. I can't get them to stop because my wife does the same thing. So,

I've decided to make my own bubblegum."

A close friend of the Conway family, John Gibbons, helped Conway pick up a washing machine just days before the incident. According to Gibbons, Conway bought the new Galaxy 773-X front-loading washing machine and said, "We have special plans for this Galaxy!"

Although police have not been able to interview Conway yet, due to his hospitalization for an undisclosed injury, they speculate that he used the Galaxy 773-X to make the bubblegum but bit off a bit more than he could chew. Neighbors called police when they noticed the pink gooey substance oozing from all the doors and windows of the modest ranch home.

22. Angela rolled her eyes. Jerome spit out the soda he was drinking. Seven-year-old Jake laughed loudly and snorted a lot while his mother shook her head back and forth. Jake's friend Sam actually fell on the floor and rolled around, holding his stomach.

23. Go, Sharks, go!
You're not slow!
We think you're great!
So activate!

24. Never count your doggie treats before they're thrown.
Unless you're the leader of the pack, your view never changes.
Greet each day with a stretch, a wiggle and a smile.

25. • Doing nothing automatically makes everyone else seem more productive, thus boosting their self-esteem.
• Doing nothing gives you time to think. A lot.
• Doing nothing helps you remember what's important in life.
• Doing nothing gives your body a break.
• Doing nothing may annoy others, thus giving you a way to get back at people who have annoyed you.

26. Her fingers were long and thin, capped by black nail polish. A tattoo of a snake wrapped around her thumb and up her wrist. On her left hand was a ring with a large green stone, etched with a drawing of a dragon breathing fire.

27. When **Carl** the **carpenter** got a job **caring** for the **carousel** at the **carnival,** he was so happy that he did a **cartwheel.** On the morning of his first day on the job, he ate a hearty breakfast filled with **carbohydrates** because his boss had told him that his first task would be to repair a couple of statues on the ride, namely the **caribou** and the **cardinal.** After fixing the statues, he went by the **caramel** corn stand and got a treat. Then he **carried** a **carafe** of water to the **caricature** artist because she looked parched. She was grateful and in turn gave him a **carnation** to wear on his shirt lapel. (Score: $140)

28. On a baby stroller: Remove child before folding.
On a garlic clove: May cause bad breath.

On a baby: May cause adults to talk in silly, high-pitched voices and make funny faces.

On a car door: Do not operate vehicle while sleeping.

On a bottle of sleeping pills: May cause drowsiness.

29. The main character in the new cartoon show, Goody-Goody Gwendolyn, is Gwendolyn the Gator. Gwendolyn may be an alligator, but she is the kindest alligator you'll ever meet. She always says, "Please," and, "Thank you," even when she's eating her prey. She always makes special trips to visit her grandpa and grandma on their birthdays, and she even goes to church with them on Sundays. Gwendolyn also enjoys singing in the church choir and organizing field trips for Sunday school students. She's the perfect role model because you would never catch her swearing or being rude in any way. You just have to pay attention because she might eat you. She doesn't mean anything personal by it, though.

30. Zookeeper Yolanda x-rays whales vigorously under the strict regimen quoted. Pandas often need more love. Kangaroos jump into hydrangeas. Giraffes find everything delicious: corn, beans, and apricots.

31. My mom's mutt Rusty won't run. Rusty trots or stops. Soon, my mom must tow Rusty.

32.   The general's orders: Get up and go mow the lawn! Now!

    The general's wife's orders: Dear, if you don't mind, could you get out of bed and come and help me with something? I'm busy cooking, cleaning, and doing laundry today, and I just don't have time to do another chore that needs to be done. Would you mind giving the grass a quick clip? It would help me out so much.

33. As I entered the kitchen, I was surprised to see smoke pouring from my dishwasher. Alarmed at the possibility of a fire burning out of control, I quickly put on some gloves and filled a bucket with water. Then I opened the dishwasher door and fanned the smoke away.

    To my dismay, the smoke kept coming, so I poured on the water. Finally, the smoke stopped. Then, to my shock, a genie popped out of the dishwasher. I was so startled that I fell backwards and dropped the bucket. The genie looked mad.

    "Why'd you go and do that?" said the genie.

    "Uh, what?!"

    "Why'd you dump that water on me?"

    "I'm sorry, I guess…I was just kind of worried about the possibility of my house burning down," I mumbled.

    "Well, I think you were being a bit paranoid. However, now that I'm standing here, I might as well give you your three wishes."

    "Really? I get three wishes? Great! My first wish is that you never spit smoke from your bottle in my dishwasher again."

    The genie sighed. "Granted."

    "Now for my other wishes…" I smiled. "Why don't you just dry off? These are going to take me a little time…"

34. Flab-Away pills aren't worth the bottle they come in. They are pure sugar, with some caffeine and other chemicals thrown in to make the ingredient list look complex. Really, any scientist will tell you that these pills won't help you lose weight. The company hopes gullible people like you will plunk down their money in the vain hope of a miracle cure for the excess pounds they have put on. There are no miracle cures for excess pounds. Flab-Away isn't going to do a thing for you—except empty your wallet.

35. Your blind date is so very kind, not only to other people, but to all creatures great and small. He is always there to lend a helping hand to his friends and acquaintances. He is polite, well-mannered, and considerate. He is always well-groomed and dresses with impeccable taste. Oh, and he likes puppies.

36. It's like your nose fills up with a thick, clay-like substance and someone pounds it in, hard, and you can't escape, no matter how hard you sneeze or blow your nose. It stays stuffed up there in your nose, and you can't get away from it, no matter what you do, despite how much it pains you and makes your eyes water and your stomach churn.

37.   "Right after my 25th win on *Jeopardy.*"
       "When television is banned from the planet."
       "As soon as aliens land on Earth in broad daylight."
       "When my Dad stops rooting for the Cubs."
       "When I win a lifetime supply of tennis shoes from Nike."
       "When celebrities in America make minimum wage."
       "When teachers in America make six-figure incomes."
       "When squirrels go waterskiing...no, wait—they have. When lizards go waterskiing."

38. Yankee Doodle was starving the day he came riding to town. After all, there were no fast food joints back then. He hadn't eaten for days and, as a result, was quite delirious. He was dreaming of his favorite dish, macaroni and cheese, drooling over the thought of gooey orange sauce covering tender noodles, when an admiring lady at the side of the road handed him a feather to adorn his hat. He had enough sense to accept the feather and put it in his cap, but when he tried to say "Thank you," all that came out was "macaroni." Before he could correct himself and explain his situation, the woman shook her head and backed off. She told everyone she knew about the strange guy who called a feather "macaroni."
       And the woman really did know *everyone*.

39.   Shannon crumpled under the pressure of the final exam in her underwater basket-weaving class.
       Harry showed up two days late to the job interview at Disneyland, wearing a crumpled tie.
       The chihuahuas crumpled to the floor after a long day of barking at every single vehicle that passed their Winnebago.

40. Lisa lost her power of speech whenever Chris was around. As she caught sight of him entering the gym, she froze and just stared. Her friend Lisa dropped her cupcake. The boys

backed off, warily, and turned around, rolling their eyes. The girls, however, cautiously approached him, smiling and blushing—that is, except for Lisa, who hadn't managed to move yet.

41. When the child ran behind the bush to get her ball, she was startled by a strange creature perched on top of the ball, staring at her. It glowed pink and had a large, black, tree-like appendage sprouting from its head. When the little girl crouched down to get a better look at the creature, it jumped into her hand.

    "Oh, do you want to be friends?" asked the little girl. The creature answered by curling up in a ball and falling asleep. At least she thought that's what it was doing. She wasn't sure with pink extraterrestrials.

    "I'm going to call you Kinkle," she said. She took Kinkle inside and made a little bed for it in her dresser drawer.

    The next day, the little girl awoke to her parents yelling. When she opened her eyes, there were giant black tree branches crisscrossing her room. Some of the branches had ripped through the walls of her bedroom. Birds sat on the branches, singing their songs as if nothing were amiss. There, on one of the branches, sat Kinkle.

42. (to the tune of "All I Have to Do Is Dream" by the Everly Brothers)

    I hate them so much, I could die.
    I hate them so, and that is why
    Whenever I see peas, all that I can do is
    screa-ea-ea-ea-eam, scream, scream, scream.

    When I see peas, I want to gag.
    When they appear, it's such a drag.
    Whenever I see peas, all I want to do is
    Screa-ea-ea-ea-eam.

    I hate them a bunch.
    Don't want them for lunch,
    Or anytime, night or day.
    Only trouble is, gee whiz,
    I'm screaming my life away.

    I hate them so much, I could die.
    I hate them so, and that is why,
    Whenever I see peas, all I want to do is
    Srea-ea-ea-ea-eam, scream, scream, scream.
    (Fade) Screa-ea-ea-ea-eam, scream scream scream.

43. My mom bought an old plum colored car and gave it to me on my 16th birthday. The engine doesn't sound too good, but the body is in good shape, smooth as an eggshell, and the seat covers are as soft as peach fuzz. It runs okay, but it has an old car smell that reminds me of moldy bread. I sure hope it doesn't turn out to be a lemon.

44. I'm all alone in the house late at night, and I hear loud wailing sounds coming up the dimly lit basement stairs, punctuated by heavy footsteps.

45. Make sure your Tonka wheels are always firmly on the ground, just like a real truck.

    The potty is specially reserved just for you to put your #1 and #2 in. Mommy's shoes go on a special shoe rack in the closet.

    Let's draw your pretty elephants on this nice paper to keep in your special picture book forever, instead of on the walls where they'll get painted over if we move someday.

46. I am one true, loyal friend—totally, honestly, genuinely.

47. Chairs have four legs because…

    …it makes them harder to knock over.

    …they are more symmetrical than they would be with three legs.

    …because any more legs would just be in the way.

    …because somebody a long time ago invented the four-legged chair and nobody's come up with anything better.

    …because with four legs, they match tables, which also have four legs.

    …because the union of chair leg manufacturers is very strong and won't let companies decrease the number of legs on chairs because the union members would have less work.

    …because nine or ten legs would just look silly.

    …because it's tradition, and no one wants to go against tradition.

48. King Kong screamed at the scurrying pedestrians. He lunged at the barking dogs as he swung at the shrieking cats. He pounded his fists on his chest and hurled hot dog vendors to the pier. He blew cars and buses out of his path. He kicked tall buildings until they fell to the ground.

49. For the most contemporary designs in light blocking and privacy blinds, choose Zebra Wink. When the Zebra Winks, you're in the dark.

50. "Stop your bellyaching and get your chores done," Mom said sternly.

    "I'm too tired," Joey whined. "Do I have to?"

    "Absolutely," Mom replied. "If you had done your chores instead of complaining, you'd be done now."

    "I know, I know, " Joey moaned. "I never do anything right. All you ever do is criticize me."

    "Poor baby," Mom said. "You suffer so."

    Joey looked up hopefully.

    Mom folded her arms and gave him a look. "Yes, my heart is breaking for you, but I'll have to cry later…after you do your chores. Now, move!"

51. Alison Krauss is undoubtedly the most unbelievably incredible fiddle playin' bluegrass singer ever to cross the Mason-Dixon line. She sings the saddest, most heartbreaking, tear-jerking love songs ever heard since the beginning of time. When she tunes up and starts singing

those sad tunes in that whispery velvet voice of hers, you can practically hear the collective heartbreak of the entire human race and feel the infinite flood of billions and billions of tears as if the stars were falling down from the heavens.

52. A clothes dryer is a large, heavy appliance commonly found in people's basements, kitchens, or utility rooms. A clothes dryer is usually accompanied by a washing machine, which is also a large, heavy appliance. A washing machine washes your clothes, and a clothes dryer dries them. A clothes dryer is a large square metal box that plugs into the wall. On the front of a clothes dryer, there is a door. Some clothes dryers have a solid metal square door, and other dryers have a round glass door. You put your clean wet clothes from the washer inside the clothes dryer and turn it on. In about 20 minutes or so, your clothes are dry. Many people buy dryer softener sheets and add them to the dryer with their clothes to make the clothes soft. You can also buy fabric softener in a liquid form, which you pour into a special compartment in your washing machine. A clothes dryer works by tumbling the clothes around and blasting hot air inside the dryer. Because clothes dryers use hot air to dry clothes, you need some type of ventilation from the dryer to the outside of the house so the hot air can escape. This ventilation usually comes in the form of a long silver tube that is attached to the back of your clothes dryer. The tube is then vented outside the house. Also, after every load of clothes, you need to clean out the lint filter. Lint is the fuzzy material that comes from the yarn and fabric of clothes, as well as the dryer sheets that people throw in with their clothes to make them soft. The agitation that occurs during washing and drying clothes causes these particles of lint to shed off the clothes and the dryer sheets. The dryer's lint filter traps pieces of lint so they don't get stuck in your dryer vent and catch on fire. You can also buy a lint brush for your dryer, which is a long silver flexible wire with a handle and plastic bristles at the end. You take the lint filter out of your dryer, then fish the lint brush down in there to catch the pieces of lint way down inside the dryer.

53. Clothes dryers are a modern convenience. Before clothes dryers, people hung their clothes outside to dry, on a clothesline. The advantage to a clothesline is that you get to dry your clothes for free. The disadvantage to a clothesline is that your clothes take longer to dry than they would in a clothes dryer. There are many different brands and types of clothes dryers. Major American brands include Maytag, Whirlpool, and General Electric. I have a very energy efficient clothes dryer that is made by a company called Eurotech. This company is a European brand. The Europeans are much more energy efficient because they live in smaller spaces and have less resources than we do, so they have to conserve more. The Eurotech brand is very energy efficient. American brands have changed the design of their dryers to be more energy efficient as costs for homeowners continue to rise. I recommend buying a more energy efficient clothes dryer because you will save a lot on your energy bills.

54. Anecdote to tell friends:

   I have to tell you this anecdote because it's unbelievable how dense some people can be. As you know, I bought a very energy efficient clothes dryer that is made by a company called Eurotech. At the time I bought the dryer, I had a roommate named

Bill. Bill lacks common sense, so when I had the clothes dryer delivered, I told him not to use it because it wasn't hooked up yet. Then I went out for dinner. When I came back, Bill told me the dryer wasn't working. I said, "Didn't you hear me tell you that it wasn't hooked up yet?" He just stared at me blankly. "What do you mean, 'hooked up'?" he said. I took him by the arm and led him into the laundry room. I pointed to the dryer, which was sitting in the middle of the room.

"By 'hooked up,' I meant, the ventilation tube isn't hooked up, and also, it's not even plugged in. See—the plug is lying right there on the floor, unplugged."

"Oh," he said. "I thought you said the dryer was energy efficient."

"It is," I said.

"Then why does it need to be plugged in?"

"What?" I said.

"If it's energy efficient, doesn't it run on batteries?"

"No, Bill," I said. "That's not what energy efficient means."

"Oh," he said.

55. fit as a fiddle, hit the hay, saved by the bell, rustle up some grub, down for the count, work like a dog, tougher than shoe leather, out like a light, stubborn as a mule, eat like a horse

My Uncle Buff is a lumberjack. He works like a dog cutting, lifting and hauling logs. All that work makes him as fit as a fiddle. After working hard all day, he sometimes collapses with exhaustion and seems like he's down for the count. Fortunately, he's usually saved by the bell—the dinner bell, that is. Then it's time to rustle up some grub. Uncle Buff eats like a horse and it doesn't matter if his steak is as tough as shoe leather. He just keeps chewing. He won't give up until he gets it all down—he's as stubborn as a mule. By the time he's through with his dinner and all that chewing, he's ready to watch a little TV and then hit the hay. He's so worn out, he's out like a light in five minutes.

56. My Uncle Buff is a lumberjack. He works like a machine, cutting, lifting and hauling logs. All that work makes him as fit as any Olympian. Still, after working hard all day, he sometimes collapses with exhaustion and looks so dead that his wife often checks to make sure he is breathing. Fortunately, hunger pangs usually bring him back to the world of the living, and he goes in search of food. Uncle Buff eats like the champion of an extreme eating challenge, and it doesn't matter what he eats, even if it's steak that is as tough as the skin of a rhinoceros. He just keeps chewing. He won't give up until he gets it all down—he's as stubborn as a toddler throwing a fit in the grocery store because he can't have a packet of Fudgy Sugar Bombs. By the time Uncle Buff is through with his dinner, he's ready to watch a little TV and then say hello to his mattress. He's always so worn out that, in five minutes he's out like a boxer who's been KO'd.

57. A ditz is a term used to describe a female who maybe isn't real smart, or at least doesn't act like it. Someone might say a girl is acting ditzy if she is walking along, talking on her cell phone, giggling, and not watching where she's going and then runs right into you and says,

"Ooooh, where did you come from?" When a person is called a ditz, it's usually because she's being silly or acting like she has no common sense at all. Sometimes it can also mean she's kind of spoiled. As another example, you might call someone a ditz if she said, "Like, I don't understand why I got an 'F' on my report on an important city in the world. I don't see what city is more important than Europe!"

58. Dear Bertha,

As you know, I have expressed feelings of love for you and would like to ask you to consider joining our mutual goals and assets in a marital union. If you would like to accept this offer, we can discuss all the pertinent details at a scheduled appointment time that is agreeable to both of us. If your response is favorable, please contact me as soon as possible, as I would like to begin planning our future together.

Faithfully yours,
Mortimer

59. If we can send a man to the moon, surely we can figure out how to send a woman to the White House.

If we can send a man to the moon, surely we can find a way to make cars run on water or some other inexpensive substance, so that we aren't dependent on the Middle East for oil.

If we can send a man to the moon, surely we can figure out a way to make health insurance affordable for everyone in the country.

If we can send a man to the moon, surely we can find a way to make cell phones shut off automatically in public gatherings.

If we can send a man to the moon, surely we can figure out a way to make television pay for itself without commercials.

60. Cats are the best thing for eliminating rats. They also make mice go away. These kitties can sometimes cause you to sneeze. They like to play with catnip-filled mice every day.

61. "Enjoy the view of those *spacious skies and amber waves of grain!*" my mom yelled as I was walking to the bus for summer camp. I was so embarrassed. A boy with a safety pin through his ear lobe laughed at me, and a girl with black fingernails and green hair rolled her eyes. As I walked by them I muttered under my breath, *"I've a feeling we're not in Kansas anymore."*

62. These days the autumn breeze from up in the trees causes everyone to sneeze. I also sneeze and wheeze when I eat cheese or Wheaties. I guess I'm allergic to these. My dog is allergic to fleas and bees. He's better off when he's catching some Z's. My mom agrees that we should not tease those who sneeze. We'll all feel better after there is a freeze.

63. Have you ever noticed how car dealers like to lure customers in to their big sales? They advertise great deals in order to reel the buyers in and give them the sales pitch. Once they hook the customer into thinking they have just the right car, they pull the old bait-and-

switch routine. The advertised deal is gone, but they have this other car, much nicer, with fancy fins and a really cool paint job. It costs a little more, but with the customer's net income, affording it is no problem. Before you know it, the car dealer has tipped the scales for the buyer and he drives away in a new car, thinking this time he's caught the big one. Sounds like a fish story to me.

64. Yesterday morning, I was hanging out as usual on the back bumper of the family car. It had been a cold night, so I was all frosted over. Finally, my owner came out to go to work, coffee in hand and eyes still at half-mast. She backed out of the drive a little too fast, whacking me on the curb. At least I knew I was awake then. She proceeded to run a stop sign in her rush to get to work on time and barely missed hitting another car. Lucky for her, no one could get my number—I was still covered in frost.

65. Lou doesn't have a clue about how to woo. He invited Pru to the zoo, but then he got the flu, turned an awful hue, and had to spend the day in the loo. When he got better, he decided to try anew. He bought some glue and made a flirty card for Pru, but he grew nervous and didn't go through with it. I think in a few more days, Lou will get his courage up and try something new. Perhaps he will figure out that Pru is due a slew of roses.

66. Dear Mr. & Mrs. Dunkle,

As I'm sure you know, Andrew is certainly a very active little boy. We are having a bit of a challenge in getting him to focus his energy on learning. For example, he's having a hard time understanding that focusing his energy on learning doesn't mean ripping up the textbooks or kicking over desks. I'm sure, with your help, we will get over this hump in his educational journey.

Andrew also has quite an advanced vocabulary. Most six-year-olds don't have words like "muddle-headed nincompoop" trip off their tongues, and he needs a bit of help in learning which of his many words are appropriate for the classroom. Perhaps we can start with helping him learn that my name is Miss Shackleford, and not Miss Dimwitted Dunderhead. There are also a few less-than-refined words he needs to learn to keep reserved for some very private part of his brain.

At lunchtime, it's clear that Andrew loves food, not just for eating, but for manipulating, so I recommend an art class as a creative outlet. Mashed potatoes on indoor/outdoor carpet is not, in my opinion, the proper medium for his talents.

Finally, Andrew needs to learn to curb his impulse to whack something whenever he hears the word, "No." He needs to learn that fellow students are not for pounding with his Nikes. He needs to learn that paste is not for eating, and chalk is not for stomping on, and paper is not for wadding up and throwing.

I look forward to working with you to help solve our special challenges with Andrew and help us all have a good year for your highly energetic little boy.

Sincerely,
Miss Shackleford

67. Penelope preened her pretty ponytail while posing with purple parrots for a picture to put on her personal postcards. She purchased pink paper to print her picture postcards on. The printing press produced plenty of practically perfect postcards for Penelope. Penelope then parked her parents' Pontiac at the post office and put her postcards in the postal box. Afterward, she picked up a pepperoni personal pan pizza and proceeded to a party. She's probably plumb pooped by now.

68. When winter sets in, our family comes alive. Winter is our favorite season because we love to ski, ice skate, snowboard, and, most of all, have snowball fights. We vote during the week to decide which activity or activities we will participate in during the upcoming weekend. Weekends are so jam-packed with outdoor activities that we hardly have time to sleep.

69. The black and white panda seems quiet today. The panda chews sugar canes. The panda loves trees. The panda hates cages. The panda looks happy.

70. photograph, physician, phone, phase, phantom, pharmacy, Phoenix, philosopher, phobia, photocopy

   When I answered the phone, my aunt said, "Hello! I just got back from my physician, who said I have a computer phobia." I suggested she try drinking some chamomile tea to calm herself down, but she didn't have any. Since she is also afraid of going to the store by herself, I said I would get some for her. While at the grocery store, I decided to pick up my prescription from the pharmacy. As I was waiting, I ran into a philosopher from Phoenix. He claims that making photocopies of photographs is a way to make yourself smarter.

   Just when I thought my day couldn't get any stranger, the school principal called and told me that she was having a problem with my brother. He refuses to go to physical education class. Apparently, he's going through a phase where he thinks phantoms are real, and believes there are ghosts in the boys' locker room.

71. Cinderella took her cell phone with her during her morning chores. She wiped down the microwave, cleaned the espresso machine and dusted the television and DVD player. That afternoon an invitation came via e-mail, inviting all the single women in the household to a dance club to meet the prince. Cinderella's wicked stepmother replied, saying all would attend except Cinderella. However, she was quickly blasted with text messages from the palace insisting that Cinderella be allowed to attend. The stepmother and stepsisters reluctantly let Cinderella get ready for the dance.

   Luckily, Cinderella's fairy godmother appeared with her magic wand to help dress the poor maiden. She swirled around the room in a flash, and soon Cinderella was dressed in Prada with Manolo Blahnik designer heels. Her fairy godmother conjured up a red Porsche for the young woman to ride in to the dance. Cinderella was warned that staying out past midnight would turn the Porsche into a scooter and her outfit back to overalls.

   Cinderella attended the club and danced with the prince most of the evening. Her cell phone alarm went off at midnight. As she broke into a run to leave the dance club before her overalls made an appearance, one of her fancy heels slipped off on the club steps.

Cinderella left in the nick of time. As she jumped in the Porsche, it turned into a scooter and left Cinderella, clad in overalls, to ride it all the way home.

The next morning an e-mail arrived announcing that the lone fancy high-heeled shoe would be making the rounds of the kingdom, in an attempt to find the owner. The prince obviously liked the woman in the hip outfit and fancy heels. He wanted to find her. A bike messenger was sent out to take the shoe to each woman in attendance the previous evening. When the heel arrived at Cinderella's house, the two stepsisters tried to cram their feet into the petite shoe, to no avail. Cinderella tried the high-heeled shoe, and it slipped comfortably over her foot. A text message was sent to her phone announcing that she was invited to meet the prince later that day for lunch. The rest is history…with a happily-ever-after ending.

72. Anchorage, Alaska, is home to the legendary astronaut, Jake Phillips. Mr. Phillips was a student of astronomy who wrote five books on the subject. In actuality, he likes to attribute his passion for space to his parents, who are from Australia. It should be no surprise that Mr. Phillips himself will be the authority at the next Astronaut Recruitment Fair. Every day during the event, Mr. Phillips and his assistant will lead audiences in an amazingly adept lecture that is sure to inspire all promising young astronauts to pursue a career in space.

73.   "The grass smells red." John looked confused as he pulled in another deep breath. Everybody around John ignored his statement. People were busy painting pumpkins and anxiously waiting for the corn maze to open. John decided to say it again, louder. "The grass smells red!"

Finally, a gentleman to his left answered him. "The grass is not dead."

"I didn't say the grass was 'dead.' I said the grass smells 'red,'" said John.

"That doesn't even make sense," replied the gentleman.

"Yes it does. The grass smells red, meaning the grass smells like blood."

"You're a strange, strange man," the gentleman said as he backed away and alerted the police on his cell phone.

74. Grandpa George always comes up with **insanely** fun things to do. Most people think he is **off his rocker** because of his **loopy** sense of humor, but I love him and his **nutty** ideas. For example, last summer Grandpa George suggested we dress up like pilgrims and canoe around the lake singing "Edelweiss." We were so bored that we agreed to this **absurd** idea. My Grandma Dotty shook her head and sighed, **"Lunatic."** Everybody knows she adores the **eccentric** man we call Grandpa. I hope I can achieve the same **wacky** outlook on life as I get older.

75. Ugly words: hate, puke, surgery, sick, phlegm, scaly, scab, slimy, putrid, terrible.

I hate phlegm. When I am sick with a cough I wish I could have surgery to remove the slimy phlegm so I don't feel like puking. I'd rather be in a skateboard crash than cough up phlegm. Of course, getting in a crash means dealing with scaly scabs. And if you're in a really bad accident, you can break your leg or arm or something, and then you will have to have a cast. Then, when the cast comes off, you will have to deal with the putrid smell—a terrible thing.

76.   "How are you doing?" asked Ted.

"You know I'm moving, right?" replied Sandra.

"What? Moving?"

"Didn't Amber tell you?"

"Was she supposed to?"

"Don't you two have study hall together?"

"She was supposed to tell me in study hall?"

"Wasn't she in study hall yesterday?"

"Didn't she leave early for a basketball trip yesterday?"

"So she didn't tell you because she was gone?"

77.   "Yipes!" said the zebra. "I've lost my stripes."

"Cripes! What's the hype?" said the horse.

"I said I've lost my stripes," said the zebra. "Now I'm a regular old horse like you."

"That's a stupid gripe," said the horse.

"Shut your windpipe!" said the zebra.

"Well, I may be a regular old horse—maybe even a stereotype, but I would rather think of myself as an archetype, if you don't mind."

"You can go play the bagpipes for all I care," said the zebra.

"Well, aren't you a guttersnipe!" said the horse. "Maybe if you had my blood type you wouldn't be so mean."

"I'm sorry," said the zebra. "I'm just so upset! My imagination is ripe with the **awful** scenarios of what it will be like to live without stripes."

"Maybe you can type a letter to the stripes people asking for the prototype for stripes. In the meantime you can wear a striped shirt and some striped tights so no one will notice you've lost them."

"Thanks, Horse. I'm sorry I took a swipe at you for being a horse. I guess I'm really attached to my stripes," said the zebra, crying.

"Wipe your tears," said the horse. "Here's a Handi Wipe."

"Thanks," said the zebra. "I haven't met a horse this nice since the days of tintype."

78. An overblown holiday in November is one I wish I could skip. Mom always makes gross green bean casserole. Dad slices pumpkin pie before dinner and drinks a bunch of coffee, which makes him nervous and on edge. My sibling Sally shoves her food in napkins and feeds our dog. Every year I am blamed for her behavior.

79. Anne's eyes grew wide when her mom set her birthday cake on the tray in front of her. She giggled as her hands squished through the icing. With her fingers covered in icing and cake, she shoved them into her mouth and giggled some more. The icing smeared across her face like clown make-up, and her hands wore gloves of cake. It would take a long bath to get the birthday cake off the toddler.

80. Bernard heard the buzz of the city all around him as he sloshed down the street. Passing cars beeped at each other in their hurried way. Bernard's boots went splat on the wet cement. He heard the loud clang of bells as he passed a church. When he reached his friend's house, he pressed the doorbell. Ding-dong! The door creaked opened and Stanley invited him in. Bernard loved the tick-tock of the cuckoo clock hanging in Stanley's front hallway. As Bernard and Stanley sat down in the living room, Stanley's cat Pickles began scratching the sofa. "No!" said Stanley. The cat hissed, then came over and purred, rubbing against Stanley's leg.

81.   Mary had a little fish,
        Little fish, little fish.
        Mary had a little fish.
        She got it in Hong Kong.

        And everywhere that Mary went,
        Mary went, Mary went,
        Everywhere that Mary went
        She brought her fish along.

        She wrote her fish some pretty prose,
        Pretty prose, pretty prose.
        She wrote her fish some pretty prose.
        She was a little strange.

        She dressed it up in fancy clothes,
        Fancy clothes, fancy clothes.
        She dressed it up in fancy clothes.
        Some say she was deranged.

        She always brought her fish to work,
        Fish to work, fish to work.
        She always brought her fish to work
        And set it on her chair.

        Her fellow workers laughed at her,
        Laughed at her, laughed at her.
        Her fellow workers laughed at her,
        But Mary didn't care.

        Mary had the last guffaw,
        Last guffaw, last guffaw.
        Mary had the last guffaw
        When she received a raise.

        Why did Mary's boss do this?
        Boss do this? Boss do this?
        Why did Mary's boss do this?
        The others were amazed.

82. My fairy godmother would look like my own mother, with black hair, blue eyes, cute dimples, and a kind smile. The reason my fairy godmother would look like my own mother is because my mom lives in another state and I don't get to see her more than a few times a year. I would want my fairy godmother to look like my mom so I wouldn't miss her so much. My fairy godmother would offer me hugs and advice. She would make special dinners for me every once in a while, like the baked macaroni and cheese topped with tomatoes that my mom makes for me when I'm visiting. My fairy godmother would help me by making me feel better when I'm down. My fairy godmother would be a very cheerful and bubbly person who would remind me that every cloud has a silver lining.

83. I look out my apartment window and see sun filtering through trees and down onto cars, making them shine. I see Mrs. Johnson leaning out her window, shaking a blue and yellow quilt. Her husband, Theodore, exits their brownstone, holding their dog Kipper on a leash.

84. Frank is as exciting as a bowl of instant mashed potatoes.
  Celeste has fingers as long as celery stalks.
  Angie's eyes are as big as Aunt Reggiano's special Sunday Italian meatballs.
  Keith is as weak as a wet noodle in the rain.
  Sarah's hair is as dark as burned cookies.
  Andy is as energetic as corn kernels popping in a giant popcorn popper at a movie theater.
  Arianne is as temperamental as my special cheese souffle—sometimes high,
    sometimes low, sometimes just right.
  Emily is as warm and friendly as freshly baked bread sitting on a sunny window sill.
  Justin is as sweet as a just-picked pineapple.
  Rory looked as pale as the undercooked sugar cookies she was pulling out of the oven.

85. As Antonio opened the door, he gasped to see…
  …his family and friends gathered around a birthday cake with lit candles, singing
    "Happy Birthday."
  …his new puppy relieving itself on his wife's favorite pair of designer shoes.
  …a masked intruder leaving a trail of blood as he fled through the kitchen window.

86. Jack liked a lake. He did feel a gale. He hiked back.

87. The tortilla tasted like old wet cardboard left out in an alley for a week.

88. Dwight and Dwayne are a couple of dwarves who used to dwell in a little hut in the forest. One day a couple of dweebs moved in next door and started chopping down all of the trees. This resulted in a dwindling supply of timber and firewood, so the dwarves had no choice but to find a new dwelling. They packed up all their belongings, including their pet dweedle bug, and drove to the city, leaving the dweebs to dwell alone in the forest.

89. It's the night of the eighth grade formal dance, and Austin's mom has volunteered to drive Austin and his best friend and their girlfriends to the dance. The boys are looking very grown up and very uncomfortable in their ties and sport jackets. The girls look lovely and shy in their fancy outfits.

All is going well when mom bursts into a raucous rendition of "Bad Boys." She's giving it all the body language she's got, bopping in time to the music, trying to look cool as she's belting out her song, a little off key. The girls roll their eyes. Austin's best friend slides his eyes over to Austin with a "Can you believe this?" look. Austin just turns beet red and sinks low in the back seat, hoping that no one he knows passes them and that she ends her song before they pull up at the school.

90. Sneaking up behind a Clydesdale horse and giving it a slap on the behind is a bad idea.
Putting on mascara while driving through rush hour traffic is a bad idea.
Using a hubcap as an umbrella in a lightning storm is a bad idea.
Entrusting your toddler to put away your fine china is a bad idea.
Giving your bank account number and password to a telemarketer selling raffle tickets for weekend getaways is a bad idea.
Asking your parents for an allowance right after you have flunked three subjects and wrecked your dad's vintage Corvette is a bad idea.
Carrying a tall stack of heavy boxes down an icy, slippery fire escape is a bad idea.
Approaching a grizzly bear with cubs to get a good photograph is a bad idea.
Letting your baby brother ride piggyback while you're downhill skiing is a bad idea.
Using a fork to get toast out of the toaster without unplugging it first is a bad idea.

91. What is the opposite of *yes*? No.
What is the opposite of *no?* Yes.
What is the opposite of *certainly?* Maybe.
Can you tell me the answer? What is the question?

92. Miss Klinkfelder watched as the junior high students in her cooking class removed their cakes from the ovens. To her dismay, all of the cakes were flat.
"Now, class, you apparently didn't follow the instructions and left an important step out. Did you add flour?"
The class replied in unison, "Yes."
"Did you add eggs?"
"Yes."
"Did you add milk?"
"Yes."
"Did you add baking powder?"
The class didn't answer. One student raised her hand. "Adding baking powder wasn't on your instruction sheet, Miss Klinkfelder."
"Don't be ridiculous," she said. "I wouldn't forget one of the most important ingredients!"
The student walked up and handed the instruction sheet to Miss Klinkfelder.
Miss Klinkfelder read the sheet. She blushed. "Oops," muttered Miss Klinkfelder.

93. After Fatima had opened all of her birthday presents, her parents announced they had one

last special present to give her. Her mother went into the other room, came back with a large box wrapped in colorful paper, and then proudly handed it to Fatima. Fatima frowned. This special present was way too small to be a car. Still, perhaps there were keys inside…

Slowly she opened the present. Inside was a brand new laptop computer. As her parents smiled happily, Fatima looked up and started crying. "It's only a laptop computer," she sobbed. "You never get me what I want!" She stomped upstairs to her room and slammed the door.

94. The phrase, "You're pulling my leg," arose from an incident that also spawned a whole body of folklore about the Loch Ness monster. It all started when young Sean McCracken decided once and for all to get out of doing a chore he hated: checking the fishing nets in Loch Ness every morning at 5:00 a.m. sharp. Sean made up a story about being attacked by a monster in the lake, hoping Uncle Patrick would see that he had been psychologically scarred and could no longer be expected to go out on the lake to check the nets. Sean told him the monster had grabbed his leg and nearly pulled him out of the boat as he was checking nets on the south side of the lake.

Sean knew his uncle well enough to know that he would want to see the monster for himself. Uncle Patrick, as Sean had expected, said, "I've been checking nets for over 50 years and I've never seen any monster."

Sean countered with, "If you don't believe me, I suggest you go see for yourself."

"Okay, I will," said Uncle Patrick. "I'll be there bright and early tomorrow morning checking the nets and waiting for your so-called 'monster.'"

The next morning, Sean woke up before Uncle Patrick and ran to the south side of the lake. He waded in until he was almost under the water, then cut a long reed to breathe through. He knew his uncle would have to dangle his legs over the boat in order to check the nets, and when he did, Sean planned to grab a leg and pull as hard as he could.

Sean waited under the water by the nets until he saw his uncle's legs dangling from the surface. Then he swam up and pulled on one of his legs as hard as he could. When he heard Uncle Patrick yelling "Help! Help!" he knew he had convinced him there was indeed a monster in the lake, so he let go and swam away, surfacing among the tall grasses where he could hide. He watched as his uncle quickly rowed the boat to shore, jumped out, and began running back to the house. Uncle Patrick told everyone his story, and soon the whole town was talking about "Nessie," the name Uncle Patrick had given the "monster."

From then on, Uncle Patrick never made Sean check the nets. Uncle Patrick didn't check them, either. Instead, Uncle Patrick assigned the chore to Sean's younger brother, Ian. After about a week of checking nets, Ian came back one day with a story about a monster, complaining that he was also afraid to check the nets.

Suddenly, without thinking, Sean burst out with, "He's lying!"

"And how would you know, laddie?" asked Uncle Patrick suspiciously.

Sean eventually had to admit what he had done. Uncle Patrick was furious, and demanded that Sean go to the village and tell every single person what he had done. Hence, the phrase, "You're pulling my leg," was born.

Incidentally, some of the villagers refused to believe the story, figuring Sean was making it up to put them at ease, and that's why the legend of Nessie lives on to this day.

95. The ringleader was arguing with the clowns again. Not one clown would agree to ride the lion "like a horsie," as the ringleader had suggested. Dabby the Clown explained to the ringleader that a lion was in no way like a "horsie" and that the trick was much too dangerous. Slappy the Clown also spoke up, saying the trick would not only be dangerous to the rider but might hurt the lion, too.

"Oh, nonsense," said the ringleader.

Rippy the Clown shot back with, "If you think it's so easy, maybe you should do it."

The ringleader replied, "I would, but it's not in my job description."

96. "Icky" is stepping barefoot on a freshly chewed wad of Bubblicious.

"Icky" is when the leftover meatloaf in the Tupperware at the back of the refrigerator is green and growing hair.

"Icky" is maggots hatching out of the fish guts in the bottom of the garbage can.

"Icky" is when your brother decides to wear the same Chicago Cubs sweatshirt every day for a month without using deodorant.

"Icky" is when your Big Guy Burger arrives with slimy, wilted lettuce and a hair hanging out of the bun.

97. Extensive research on a cure for hiccups has concluded that swallowing a half-cup of seawater followed by a cinnamon roll will instantaneously stop this annoying affliction. According to Dr. Philip C. Wrangler, the cure for hiccups may sound a bit crazy, but it certainly works. He says he has begun advising his patients with chronic hiccups to follow the seawater and cinnamon roll cure and has had amazing results. "It really works," says Dr. Wrangler. "Apparently the seawater acts as a moistening agent for the diaphragm, relaxing the muscle. Then the cinnamon in the cinnamon roll stimulates the diaphragm one last time, essentially interrupting the hiccup cycle. Finally, the dough from the cinnamon roll refocuses muscle activity in the stomach, diverting stimulus away from the diaphragm."

98. Bartholomew arrives home from his job as CEO of Yuppie Records, starts to brush off his camel hair coat, but then remembers he has a butler to do such things. He calls for Geoffrey and sits down as the butler brushes the coat and hangs it in the walk-in coat closet. Then he has Geoffrey slip off his Italian leather shoes and wipe them with a chamois cloth before putting them in his walk-in shoe closet.

After changing into a cashmere work-out suit, Bartholomew goes to the kitchen to ask his personal chef to prepare dinner. He requests lobster thermidor with a salad of imported salad greens and French cheese. While waiting for dinner, he retires to his home movie theater with a glass of champagne.

99.   The ocean would look red, since its color is a reflection of the sky. All maps would, therefore, have red oceans.

The phrase, "blue skies" would never appear in the dozens of songs and poems it appears in today.

Romantics would never utter: "Your eyes are as blue as the sky."

No one would ooh and aah over red sunsets, since a red sky would be nothing special.

Sailors wouldn't be able to distinguish between a red sky at night or a red sky at morning.

100.   That low-slung little pooch of yours certainly has a unique and eye-catching haircut. And what a solid, sturdy little guy he is! His legs may not be overly long, but they certainly do get him around. And, my, what discriminating taste he has! He is *very* particular about what he eats. You'll never have to send him for training in assertiveness, either. The little guy isn't at all shy about letting you know what he needs or wants, or even when he is displeased about something. And he's smart. When he wants attention, he's bright enough to show you clearly what he wants! What a pooch!

101.   The chicken crossed the road to feast on delicate strands of wheat.
The chicken crossed the road to escape the farmer who was chasing it with an ax.
The chicken crossed the road to elope with the rooster of her dreams.
The chicken crossed the road to seek her fortune at the farm down the road.
The chicken crossed the road to escape the representative from Chicken Nuggets R Us.

102.   My new puppy is THE most adorable little thing. She has the cutest little paws, especially with the pink nail polish I use on her. She looks so precious in her little lace sweater and bow—they PERFECTLY match the pink nail polish. She is so cute I just want to squeeze her in a big hug CONSTANTLY!

I got her a little china plate for her puppy chow. I take her for walks twice a day with her rhinestone leash that matches her rhinestone collar, and I'm just SO proud when people stop and admire her. I also got her a pink velvet puppy bed to sleep in when I'm gone. At night, she cuddles up on the pillow next to my head. It is SO **sweet!** I am the luckiest girl in the world to have found this little darling!

103.   The orfinbellydorper is a highly sophisticated device used to attract salamanders. The orfinbellydorper impersonates a salamander sunning itself on rocks during the summer and sends out a slight vibration to signal to other salamanders that the area is safe. Switch the orfinbellydorper on and place the device on a rock in the sun. Soon you will enjoy seeing many salamanders sunning themselves next to the orfinbellydorper.

104.   Brittany set the first casserole she had ever made on the table. She was so proud she felt like putting a little sign with her name on it in front of the dish.

She grabbed a chair close to the buffet table so she could watch what people put on their plates and keep an eye on the ones who took her casserole. She settled into a black beanbag chair and listened to her friend Jessica chatter on and on about the cute guy in the backyard by the picnic table, but Brittany only half-listened. She didn't even pay much attention to the cute guy, although he was very cute and just her type.

Suddenly she saw someone put a scoop of her casserole on his plate. She didn't know how he'd managed to get inside without her noticing, but it was the cute, dark-haired guy. Her face lit up. A cute guy was going to be the first to taste the casserole! She watched him closely because she wanted to see where he would sit.

But just as the guy put the green bean casserole on his plate, he said loudly, "What is this??? My plate is ruined! Who the heck doesn't know that you are supposed to drain the green-bean water out of the green beans before you put them in a casserole!!! Look at this mess!!!"

Jessica jumped up to give him another plate as Brittany burst into tears. She slipped from the room and went into the bathroom, where she sobbed and sobbed. Her first attempt at cooking had been a failure.

105. What did the police officer say to the lady who was double parked while she ran into the bank for just a minute to get some cash before taking her granddaughter shopping at the new retail center?

> Hit the road,
> Or be towed.

106. What did the soccer mom say when giving her son James a ride to school and James turned the radio to his favorite station, which was playing a song with lyrics so offensive that she stopped the car in horror?

> If that's a song,
> That's WRONG!

107. Never hug a porcupine.
Never dye shorts in the turkey roasting pan.
Never try for a close-up snapshot of a skunk.
Never press "delete" when you're dealing with your hard drive.
Never send eggs through the mail.
Never eat the skin of a kiwi or a sweet potato.
Never ride your bike in the dark wearing Goth clothing.
Never buy a nosebleed seat at the baseball stadium, especially if you're prone to getting nosebleeds.
Never drive at night without turning on your headlights.
Never feed a crocodile cookies.

108. Jack and Jill were a brother-sister team of professional bobsledders who climbed up a hill near their mountain lodge to retrieve some water for their dog Skamp. Skamp was in desperate need of fresh mountain water—the water at the lodge just wasn't good enough for him.

However, Jack tripped on his new boots and fell, rolling down the hill. Jill tried to grab him but tripped and came tumbling down after him. As Jack fell, his head slammed against a protruding tree branch, and he broke his crown. Though it looked serious, it wasn't that bad. A few stitches later, he was home. Jill, who had not been injured, welcomed him with hot tea and a disappointed Skamp, who still wanted some fresh mountain water.

109. I paid a visit recently to the local junkyard, searching for some spare parts for my wrecked car. Apparently a skunk had visited recently as well because the place stunk to high heaven. The proprietor, who appeared to be slightly drunk, managed to scrounge up a couple of spare parts covered in a thick layer of putrid smelling gunk. My stomach reeled and I promised myself that the next time I came searching for parts, I would not dunk day-old greasy donuts into my coffee on my way over.

110.   IM FARMR
       LUV FRMG
       LVTOFRM

111.   My, but isn't this festive looking—the colors of Christmas!
       This is certainly an interesting combination of ingredients.
       Why, I'll bet this is just loaded with antioxidants.

112. Brooke's front tooth is loose and she is anxious to lose it. She desperately wants the good tooth fairy to visit her room on the second floor. One evening, Brooke settles down with her favorite book, *Molly Moose and the Rusty Rooster Shoot Hoops,* and a big bowl of strawberry ice cream. Her dog sits at her feet and drools. As Brooke eats the cool treat, she hits her loose tooth with the spoon. "Oops," she thinks. She runs to the bathroom, kicks the door open, runs to the mirror, and tries to pry her tooth out. It still isn't loose enough. To boost her spirits, she goes to the front stoop to watch the neighborhood kids play in the street. She feels cooped up. She feels like pulling a hood over her head because the tooth fairy will pass over her house again.

113. I'm really sorry my mother planted pink geraniums in these pots on the porch. I really like red ones so much better, don't you? In fact, if it were me, I wouldn't plant geraniums at all. I'd choose some kind of wild flowers. I think wild flowers are so cool, especially when they're in the wild. But they would be cool in flower pots, too.

   I see you washed your car. It looks a lot better. My dad says you can tell a lot about a person by the state of his car. I guess "dirty" isn't a very good thing to say about a person, so I'm glad you washed it. Did you use that new car wash down on Seventh? I saw it was open, but I think it's fifty cents more than the one over on Ninth. Maybe it's better though, or faster, or something. They must do something to justify fifty cents more.

   At least you have a car. I sure wish I did. My dad says that having a car is a privilege, not a right, and as soon as I can pay for one myself, along with the insurance and gas, I can have one. Well, that's not going to be any time soon. I wish he was like Monica's folks. They bought her a car for her sixteenth birthday, and it wasn't even a clunker or anything like yours. I don't think she even knows how lucky she is.

Well, she's not lucky in all ways. She does have fat ankles. I mean, have you ever seen her in a skirt? Probably not, since she hardly ever wears one. That's because of her ankles. You can see them when she wears cropped pants or shorts in gym. They're bad, very bad. Very fat.

It's weird because the rest of her isn't fat. Maybe it's genetic or something…you know, like brown eyes or freckles. I'm sure glad I didn't inherit my dad's freckles. My sister did—but at least they aren't real dark like his. In fact, they're kind of cute.

Speaking of cute, I do think you're cute. Really cute. I guess that isn't the word guys like to hear. I suppose you'd rather hear something like "hot" or "handsome," but girls always say "cute," at least to each other. It's a good thing, you know.

Oh, you vacuumed the car, too. Cool! I like it a lot better. Last time there were all these little crumbs in the seat, like you had been eating potato chips or something. I guess they didn't leave little grease spots, though, so it must not have been potato chips. Maybe it was cookies…

114.   Hope will stay here.
Send your blue book.
Will your rose grow?
Gwen came back home.

115. "Oh, man! That concert last night was righteous. My bro and I kicked it and didn't jam out of there until after midnight. It cost me plenty of dough to buy a hip t-shirt, and that bummed me out big time. Dude, I about wigged out when I saw the price, but it was so cool I had to have it. The next concert we go to, we gotta roll up in a tight car and hook up with our bros."

116. "How am I, you ask? Well, I could be a lot better. For one, my car has been in the shop for weeks. I've had to ride the bus to work every day. I hate riding the bus because it's so crowded. Also, I have to leave work two hours earlier than usual just to make it on time to work because the bus takes forever. So, I have to get up at 5:00 a.m. to make it to work by 8:00 a.m. That's not easy to do, especially considering that my new neighbors have been keeping me up late at night with their loud parties. And even if I could sleep through it, I can't because I have a pain in my big toe that has been keeping me up at night. The pain just keeps getting worse and worse. My doctor says it's the shoes I'm wearing, but I've been wearing the same style of shoes for years. I'm thinking of getting a new doctor. Good doctors are so hard to find, you know. I got rid of my last one when he started going on and on about hypochondria, and I knew the guy just didn't know what he was talking about."

117. I'm moving to New York City as soon as I can save up some money. I know I need to get a job to earn money, but the jobs in this town are so boring. Instead of getting one, I plan to hang out at the mall and play my guitar and pretend to be blind so people will throw money in my guitar case. It doesn't matter that I only know two chords and can't sing.

People will still give me money because I'll try to look real pathetic. Then, as soon as I get enough money, my boyfriend, the Cruncher, and I are going to get going. He's pretty sure he can get a job on Wall Street if he doesn't wear the shirt with the skull on it. We hear that stock breaking pays real good. He thinks I'll get a job, easy, as a concierge at a fancy hotel, especially if I don't do the blind routine at the interview.

118.   Free verse:
Wondering what makes the cake so moist?
Wondering why the chicken salad is so yummy?
Wondering why the potato salad is so scrumptious?
Mayonnaise, the special sauce.

Rhymed:
Mayonnaise, mayonnaise—creamy stuff.
Can't seem to ever get nearly enough.
Hamburgers, hot dogs and grilled cheese too,
Who cares if mayo's not good for you?

119. When Carter drove his beloved truck down the road, all people could see were the wheel hubs as he sped by. If they pulled up in a parking lot beside his truck, they were sometimes tempted to park right under it, for protection, if it was raining.

Carter loved the bright yellow color of his truck, and he loved its shiny chrome roll bar and the handpainted "Yellow Fever" along the door, shooting flames toward the tinted windows.

What Carter liked best, though, was the hot tub in the back. It was nestled beneath the side boards, hidden from view. When he drove down the road, steam rose from the truck bed, making it look as if his truck was really smoking. If he had friends in the tub, he sometimes liked them to howl out in pain, as if the truck were devouring them.

Carter got a kick out of that.

120. The fumes emanating from my brother's room were so strong that my mother finally snapped. In a failed effort to show that she didn't care, she had let my brother be as messy as he wanted in his room. My mom is known for her super-sensitive nose, and finally she just couldn't take it anymore. She marched down to his room with a snow shovel and a barrel-sized trash can. She flung the mattress off of the bed frame and gasped. To her horror, she discovered rotten rinds of watermelon and a hard piece of pepperoni pizza sandwiched in the middle of an overdue library book. She sniffed out an Easter basket full of seven-month-old hard boiled eggs. She also uncovered athletic socks stiff with dried sweat and my brother's swimming towel, crawling with mildew. Last, but certainly not least, my mom found an orange, green with mold, stuck inside one of my brother's basketball shoes.

121. Come on over to surprise Roy Robertson! Roy turns 60 on the Fourth of June 2006. Follow the enclosed directions to 1610 Fellows Court. 6:30 p.m. on the dot. Be sure to

bring your most cherished dessert, too! Hope to see you there.

122. At Diamond Dog Sitting, your canine gets gourmet meals, bottled water, a cashmere dog bed, massage, and tender loving care.

123. I'll never forget that night my sister, your Aunt Ida, decided to elope with your Uncle Herb—only he wasn't your uncle then. He was just Herb. Actually, he wasn't your anything yet because you weren't even born! But anyway, it was a dark and stormy night, which is kind of ironic since Ida used to be afraid of the dark when she was a little girl. She would always run to my room when she'd wake up in the middle of the night, and I'd have to carry her back to her room and put her back to bed. She slept in a big four poster bed—actually, the one that's now in her and Uncle Herb's bedroom. You should have seen us trying to get that bed up the stairs when she talked her mom and dad into giving it to her. It took five of us three hours to get it in there, and even then we put several dents in the wall and stripped off a lot of paint.

But anyway, Aunt Ida and Uncle Herb ran off to get married that dark, stormy night after Herb got laid off from his job as a used car salesman. He had been working at Ford's A+ Used Cars. I always liked Fords, though our dad didn't think much of them. My favorite was a Ford Thunderbird. I used to drive a T-bird back when I was a senior at Smallville High School, though my dad never could understand why I bought it. It was used, of course. Real used.

But anyway, your Aunt Ida and Uncle Herb both ran off, and as soon as Dad realized she was gone, he took off in his Chevy truck. He didn't take a gun, and it's a good thing because he looked madder than I've ever seen him. He didn't track Ida and Herb down until three days later, and by then they had been married for three days and there wasn't much he could do. He was ready to accept the marriage, until he found out Herb didn't even have a job. Then he…

Well, actually, I think I don't need to be sharing the rest of the story with you, at least not until you are a whole lot older!

124. Little Kaitlyn brought her shoes to Mom as they were getting ready to go shopping. "Oh, you found your shoes! Awesome!" said Mom, slipping them on Kaitlyn's feet. As they headed for the door, Kaitlyn picked up a toy that had fallen on the floor. "Awesome!" said her mother. Kaitlyn hopped into her car seat, and her mother said, "Awesome!"

While they went through the store, with Kaitlyn strapped properly in the basket, Kaitlyn sang the ABC song. "Awesome!" said Mom. When Kaitlyn read "Count Chocula" on the cereal box, her mother said, "Awesome!" When she pointed to a doll and read "Malibu Barbie" on the box, her mother said, "Awesome!" When they pulled up to the checkout counter, Kaitlyn said, "I want to pay," and her mother said, "Awesome," letting Kaitlyn hand the cashier the money.

When Mom and Kaitlyn finally took their items and left the store, the cashier breathed a sigh of relief. "They're gone," she said. "Awesome!"

125. The dog Spot sat on the mat and chewed on his milk bone snack, while Boots the cat slept on her back with her feet in the air. When Boots woke up, she crept up to Spot and

pushed her nose in his fur while she purred. Spot gave her a lick and knocked her off her feet, so she went to her bed and fell back to sleep.

126. Quenton felt queasy after eating quince and quail. He knew he should have eaten a sandwich at his favorite deli, but he had let his friend talk him into eating at the new quintessential gourmet place for lunch. He should have questioned the quality of the restaurant, but he didn't want to start a quarrel. On top of feeling sick, Quenton was also late for his meeting with Queen Ludmilla. He cursed himself as he quickened his pace. As a reporter, he had an appointment to meet with the new queen and take down quotes from her about the birth of her quintuplets. He began to quiver. That's it—I'm quitting for the day, thought Quenton. I'm going home to crawl under my quilt.

127. Mac practiced his smile while gazing at himself in the mirror. He tried a slow smile, a leering smile, a friendly smile, a knowing smile. Then he tried some nods—a slow, thoughtful nod, a satisfied nod, a happy nod, a powerful nod. He turned to the left, and then to the right, checking out his profile and smoothing down a stray hair. He winked, then turned to the side, winking again, only a little slower this time. Nodding his head then—a satisfied kind of nod—he smiled and turned off the light.

128. Son, when your mom and I met, she was a klutz. I'm sorry to be so blunt, but **klutz** is the only word for it. When we would go out dancing, she'd have to sit at the side and watch while I danced with others. If she went out on the floor, ambulances always had to be called.

BUT…one night your mom decided there was one dance she was sure she could do—the hokey pokey. I sighed and joined her on the floor. Well, she put her left foot in okay, and she shook it all about okay. Same with her right foot and her left arm and her right arm. I started to relax. But then she put her whole body in and she shook it all about. People started flying every which way as she knocked into them. Finally, the floor was cleared, and there was no one there but your mother. That's when I looked at her and knew she was one of a kind. She looked so adorable sitting there surrounded by people crying and grabbing their elbows and knees, I just had to ask her to marry me.

When our first child came along, we knew we had to name you in honor of that special dance. That, Hokey Pokey, is your history, and I hope you can be proud of it.

129. Want to know what single personal care item will make it less likely that girls will grimace and leap back when you try to kiss them?

Want to know the secret to my long, long marriage?

What helps, though doesn't cure, the effects of Uncle Roberto's garlic and onion tomato sauce?

Sissy, since you dropped your toothbrush in the toilet, do you know what you can use instead to help your mouth feel fresh?

What did Emory accidentally pour on his cut knee, instead of peroxide?

130. Late yesterday, police were called to the scene of an altercation at the Palisades Bar and Grille. According to eyewitnesses, a fight broke out during the Battle of the Grunge mara-

thon concert being held at the Palisades this weekend.

Witnesses described a short, stocky man about 50 being chased by an assailant covered in cake crumbs and frosting. The assailant was allegedly pummeling the victim with drumsticks. According to the owner of the Palisades, the victim had entered the bar carrying a cake and accusing the performers of interfering with his cake baking business next door. The loud noises, the baker said, were causing his cakes to fall.

Bystanders report that, following a verbal dispute with a drummer, the baker threw the cake at the musician, prompting the drummer to attack the baker and chase him out into the street.

Both men were arrested and charged with disorderly conduct. The baker was reportedly treated at a local emergency room for minor cuts and scrapes.

131.   "Why can't we just get some tattoos or something?" asked Joe uneasily.

"I already told you why." Amber looked at her watch.

"Remind me." Joe was not fond of rings, and couldn't envision himself wearing one every day for the rest of his life. He didn't even want to **think** about the commitment involved.

Amber had stayed up the previous night making sketches of the ring she had always dreamed of wearing. She knew the artist would agree that her design was perfect. She also knew that the man she was about to marry could not possibly be serious when he said, "Remind me." She decided to ignore him.

She said, "The ring maker will be here in ten minutes."

132.   Penelope's Prickly Eggplant: Not your ordinary eggplant! Eggplant that has been steamed over a slow fire for hours has been sprinkled with kiwi skins, to give your tongue a wonderful prickly sensation. Served with a chili garlic sauce and freshly braised blueberries, this eggplant is one dish that will stick with you all day long.

Pickled Beef and Catfish Pie: A yummy Penelope original! Beef is stewed in dill pickle juice for several days to infuse the beef with the taste of dill, and then it is combined with fried catfish in a delicate prune and cabbage sauce. A lovely cornmeal crust is baked over all and then topped with homemade goat cheese and maraschino cherries. Truly a dish you will long remember!

Desert Dessert: A dessert sure to delight the pickiest of dessert lovers. A mound of thickly sliced jalapenos is smothered with a creamy caramel and pecan sauce and accented with freshly harvested Arizona cacti needles, offering our guests a Penelope original to be talked about for years.

133.   Sad, sorry Stan stole a shabby shawl for Sweet Sally Sample so she's sure not to shiver at her shellfish store.

134.   After taking the two-ton treasure to the tournament, a troubled trooper threw twenty turnips, trying to topple the turquoise trophy.

135.   The lamp his nephew had built out of an old banjo sported logos from all the top hockey

teams, topped with a Kool-Aid stained shade with sequins around the edge.

136. My Dear Gracie,

    I have watched you grow into such a beautiful cat and admire your zest for life and running up and down the stairs. I am happy that you are enjoying your life even though you can't go outside. You have been an excellent role model for the new kitty and I really appreciate your willingness to show him the ropes.

    Recently, you have acquired a new habit, a destructive habit that I am concerned about. The new rug in the living room seems to have grabbed your attention and sparked your interest. I have noticed you pulling on the nice rug and rolling yourself in to it. Also, I hear you clawing on the rug as if it were your scratching post.

    Gracie, this rug is a wonderful addition to the household and I'd like for you to stop destroying it. How can I help you stop scratching and pulling on the rug? I hope we can find a solution to this new destructive behavior.

    Please let me know when you are available to discuss the situation. I look forward to working with you on this matter.

    All the best,
    Jill Jelly

137. "Okay, I did it," said the prisoner, "but I'm not sorry. I'm only sorry I got caught. I really wanted that jewelry and that plasma TV. I can't afford one, and I was only trying to get what I would have if the world wasn't against me."

138. When the beautiful woman in the fancy dress walked in to the crowded party, everyone noticed. She had nice skin, long hair, and long legs. She looked sad, however. She sat in a quiet corner all by herself.

139. When the statuesque model in the tight, sequined dress walked into the animated bustle of the party, everyone stared. She had glowing, bronze skin, flowing black hair, and legs so long and shapely that every woman in the room suddenly felt frumpy. As she sat in a quiet corner all by herself, she looked sad, with downcast, tear-filled eyes.

140. A middle-aged former hippie, still sad about having to give up his Volkswagen bus, plowed his PT Cruiser into a semi truck. The impact ruined the PT Cruiser and sent the former hippie to the hospital. A show-off taking his first turn at driving an ambulance drove too fast and ignored a red light. At the same time, a cute little thing, whose father was letting her take his Porsche for a spin, also ignored the red light and hit the ambulance. Luckily, she survived the wreck, and so did the ambulance driver and the former hippie.

141. The new teacher sitting at her desk slowly looked up at the class. She cleared her throat carefully several times and then, in a voice so soft the students could barely hear her, said, "Excuse me. Excuse me." Students giggled a bit and kept right on talking. The teacher suddenly raised her voice, jumping up to reveal her black belt. She leapt onto the desk, and yelled, "DID I STUTTER?!"

142. A video game is a form of entertainment; people play video games to have fun and relax.

Remember when you used to play stick-ball in the street? It's the same concept. Fun! The video game is played on a special device that is plugged in to a television. The video game is viewed on the television's screen and manipulated by controls that players hold in their hands. For example, if the video game you are playing is about people building houses and your character is the electrician, you walk your character through the house by moving the controller in your hand. If your character needs to pick up wire, cut wire, or hang lights, then you need to move your character around like a real person to finish the task. The goal of the video game is different for each game and is dictated by the people who write it.

143.   If you ever have the notion
    To try a tasty potion,
    A fruity combination
    Brings instant gratification.

144.   "So, what did you find out?"
    "No kidding?! Orange or red?"
    "What? I prefer orange."
    "Do you think there'll be any problems?"
    "Me, too. I think there might be limited access."
    "Canada? That might not be a bad idea."
    "Okay, I'll do it."
    "Not too long."
    "That depends on the rate."
    "Enough for three months."
    "I'll get right on it. Ciao."

145. If you could chew blue, it would taste refreshing and cool, like a gust of clean ocean air.

146.   One year and six months ago our basketball team managed to win, in Denver, the state championship tournament, a contest created by the previous coaches and dedicated to the idea that teamwork is the secret to success.

    One week and two days ago, the justice of the peace officiated at the marriage of my sister to a trapeze artist, changing the meaning of the phrase "love at first sight" to "love at first flight."

    Eight years and many tears ago, my pet salamander passed into the great beyond and left me a broken mess, blubbering about my loss and vowing never again to take on the responsibility of a pet.

147. Our car would not have a very smooth ride, as it would clunk along the road with its square tires. Our CD player would have to be redesigned for rectangular CDs. Basketball, golf, volleyball and softball would probably not be popular sports. Bagels and biscuits would be square. Hamburgers would be square everywhere, not just at Wendy's. Songs like "Rock Around the Clock" would make no sense.

148. On Thanksgiving day, we love to stuff ourselves with turkey, dressing, mashed potatoes,

gravy, cranberries and pumpkin pie.

149. My super hero is Proper Paula. Proper Paula intervenes when someone displays bad manners. She has the ability to cast spells that make people behave. For example, when people rudely yell at store clerks for no reason, Proper Paula appears and puts a spell on them that makes them apologize. When people butt into lines, Proper Paula is there to send them to the back, where they belong. Drivers who tailgate or cut people off suddenly find themselves stranded in a sputtering car, thanks to Proper Paula. She also appears when people talk loudly on cell phones in restaurants. She turns their cell phones into bread rolls, which they then must politely serve to others at their table. If they behave nicely for the rest of the meal, she will return the phones, but only if they apologize and promise to behave more considerately in the future.

    And if someone should talk back to Proper Paula? She quite unceremoniously turns them into bed bugs.

150. The rich smooth gravy had a robust aroma and a creamy texture.

151. Madison skips into her classroom to share her good news. She beams at the kids—even those who always make fun of her—and laughs to herself. The other students can't help staring at her. What has happened to her normal scowl? Finally, one child asks, "What's with you, anyway? Have you won the lottery or something?"

    Madison nearly sings her answer. "I'm going to Disney World! Next week! My dad has business there, and he's taking the whole family!" She twirls into her seat and glows. "I can't wait!"

152. Zeus can save worms.

153.   The cat ate raw meat.
        The cat's ears were wet.
        The man heard the cat.
        The cat ate cream.
        The meat tastes raw.
        The cat sat near the rat.
        The cat ate treats.
        The seats were red.
        The seats were wet.
        We heard the tram.
        We saw the tram.
        The rat went there.
        The cat went where the rat went.
        The man went west.
        The Western man ate the meat.
        The dream was sad.
        The men traded the same dart.
        The car started.

That car went west.

The man's tears were sad.

That man wears a tan hat.

The mat was wet.

The heated meat wasn't raw.

A rat darted near the ram.

A cat sat near the hat.

The theme was sad.

The men made darts.

The cat wasted the treats.

The men sent cards.

The ram ran near the stream.

Her heart was sad.

154. Bill Gates: Hi, Great-great-grandpa Gates. It's your great-great-grandson Bill, speaking to you across the time barrier. I'm sitting here with my laptop, working on our family tree and wanted to ask you some questions.

Grandpa: Hi, Bill, nice to meet you. But what do you mean, sitting with your laptop? Your lap is always on top when you're sitting.

Bill: No, no. My laptop is my portable computer that I take everywhere.

Grandpa: You mean like an abacus? What's that got to do with family trees?

Bill: Never mind. Hold on a second, my Blackberry is buzzing.

Grandpa: What?! You have a buzzing blackberry? Maybe there's a bee stuck in it. Quick, throw it back in the bushes.

Bill: No, no. My Blackberry sends my e-mails to me directly from the Internet.

Grandpa: You mean a bee brings your mail to you in some kind of net? I don't see how a bee is strong enough to carry much of anything...

Bill: No, no. Forget that. Let me just record this number in my Palm Pilot.

Grandpa: Is that some kind of compass?

Bill: No, it's like an electronic daytimer.

Grandpa: You mean some kind of fancy calendar?

Bill: This isn't going so well. Forget the family tree. I think I'll just listen to my iPod.

Grandpa: You're going to listen to a bean? (*Shaking his head.*) Buzzing blackberries? Bees delivering mail? Son, are you all right? You know, I really do worry about the genes that may have gotten mixed into my family over the years...

155. Hi! Yes, my boss is still as lame as ever. You won't believe the STUPID thing he did today! He can be so dumb sometimes. I mean, hello!! Earth to Mr. Byers! So, anyway, our receptionist was out sick today and I was busy taking orders over the phone, so Mr. Byers had to make his own copies. And guess what he did! He managed to run off 237 blank sheets of paper. What an idiot! I mean, it's like, how long has he been in business, and he still doesn't know how to make copies? Hello! I mean, a monkey could probably figure it

out faster than my boss. But you gotta remember—this is the guy who tried to make coffee without putting any water in the coffee maker. At least the firemen who came were cute—or should I say HOT!

156.   The storm flooded the highway.
         The deluge engulfed the town.
         Rain came in a torrential downpour.
         The snow accumulation was five inches today.
         As temperatures fell, rain turned to sleet.
         Hail stones fell from the sky, completely covering the ground, like snow.
         The rain didn't let up until the city was flooded.
         The sky sobbed rain, like Aunt Tilly when she discovered no one like her stuffed
            bell peppers.
         The clouds spit large, random raindrops.
         Like a magnet, the hot dirt seemed to pull the rain out of the clouds.
         The large, lacy snowflakes fluttered to the ground.
         The sky vomited rain in large, spontaneous explosions of water.

157. A white-faced mime robbed the Sunny Farms Assisted Living Center yesterday afternoon, without saying a single word. He got away with a large tray of tater tot casserole, Clarissa Finnegan's extra-large fuschia geraniums, and a supersized tin of Werther's candy.

      According to head nurse Emily Fenster, the mime was able to get past the front desk by winning the receptionist over with his especially good pantomime of climbing a rope. The receptionist thought he was part of that afternoon's entertainment. Since most of the residents were attending a Karate for Life class, the mime was able to slip in and out of rooms undetected after he left the receptionist's desk.

      Described as a male about five-and-a-half feet tall and 145 pounds, the mime was wearing a full-body black jumpsuit with a large white zipper and bow tie. His face was painted white with tiny black triangles under and over each eye. If you have any information on this or other local crimes, please call Crime Stoppers at 555-5555.

158. Mrs. Marvel never missed an opportunity. After a few minutes had passed and it was clear the the elevator wasn't going to be moving anytime soon, she decided to speak to the rather scary looking teenager and the older woman trapped with her.

      "So, how are both of you today?" she said brightly.

      "Duh!" said the teenager, showing a large stud in his tongue. Mrs. Marvel wondered if it matched the one in his eyebrow and the one in his nose. Did they come as a set, she wondered, like the pearl necklace and earrings Mr. Marvel had given her for their anniversary?

      "We're stuck in an elevator. How fine can we be?" continued the teenager.

      "I'm going to be late for choir practice, and I don't know how the choir is going to get along without my organ music," said the woman holding a hymnal. "But I suppose they are just going to have to make the best of the situation."

"Yes, that's the way the cookie crumbles," said Mrs. Marvel. "And speaking of cookies, are any of you familiar with Mrs. Marvel's cookies?"

The teenager rolled his eyes. "No."

"Yes," said the woman with the hymnal. "Someone brought them to our last church potluck. I didn't eat any, though. I heard they are *really* fattening."

"Well, you'd better avoid them then," mumbled the teenager, eyeing the woman's large hips.

"I wouldn't call them 'fattening,' per se," Mrs. Marvel hurried on. "Rather, they are a decadent treat to be enjoyed in moderation."

"Decadent treat?" sniffed the teenager.

This sales pitch wasn't going as well as Mrs. Marvel had hoped. "Yes, decadent treat. Sometimes we all need to spoil ourselves." She whipped open her bag. "My Oatmeal Chunkie Chews are a delicious treat for anyone, and they are only $15.00 a box!"

"Are you offering us some?" said the teenager. "I'll be happy to eat one and let you know how decadent a treat it is."

"Well, no, but I am offering to *sell* you a box."

The woman with the hymnal sighed and turned her eyes heavenward. "Some people would look at this as an opportunity for sharing," she said, "not for making money off of fellow sufferers."

"We're not suffering!" said Mrs. Marvel.

The teenager looked at her and scratched his tattooed earlobe. "Speak for yourself, lady."

159. Louise enjoys eating banana splits during movies. Others prefer peanut butter treats. Eating during movies causes really sticky mouths. Surely the viewer should expect drinks before cinema snacks. Coffee almost always brings relief.

160. Once upon a time, a mother was very tired one morning and just wanted to put on her comfy slippers and snuggle up with a book. Her three young children, however, had question, after question, after question that morning:

"Mommy, how come they don't put Elmo on the quarter?

"Mommy, how does water get in the pipes?"

"Mommy, is Shaq a giant or are giants actually bigger than Shaq?"

"Mommy, why does the wind blow?"

"Mommy, how old do you have to be to be *old?*"

The mother's tongue soon felt numb from answering so many questions with her tired brain. Finally, when her son asked, "Mommy, how did you get so smart?" she decided *not* to tell him it was by doing well in school, always finishing homework, and going away to college. She looked outside, searching for an answer, and saw the mulberry bush in the backyard. "It came from running around a mulberry bush," she said.

"Mulberry bushes are brilliant and wise... It can work for you, too, you know. If you go outside and run around the mulberry bush, singing, you will learn all of the answers to all of your questions."

The children decided to give it a try. Thankful, the mother poured a cup of coffee and curled up with her book, hoping for at least a few moments of peace and quiet.

161.   A teenager to a parent: "Mom, I load the dishes in the dishwasher every night, make my bed every morning and take Buttercup for a walk every afternoon. I do all of this work around here, so the least you could do is pay for a new snowboard."

A bank robber to a teller: "Clear out your drawer and no one gets hurt. Believe me, this isn't just a finger I'm pointing under my jacket."

A woman to her ex-husband: "You are required—by law—to pay for our children's medical bills. Since Tory's nose job does qualify as a medical procedure, you **will** pay the bill!"

A couple to a loan officer at a bank: "Well, sir, we really need the money to finance a retreat for unwanted crocodiles. It's our dream."

A policeman to a driver: "Sir, pay the ticket now or go to court."

A dissatisfied customer to a store owner: "When I bought this turtle, you assured me that he would be a good companion. He's not. All he does is sit inside his shell all day, so I demand a full refund!"

A man who walked into a glass door to the concierge: "That's the second time this has happened. You need to put a sign on this door! And you are paying for my broken glasses!"

162.   Andy drove all night to get home. By the time he reached the toll bridge, he needed to eat. Candy stashed in the glove box would not satisfy his hunger. Deciding to find a burger joint, Andy pulled off the freeway. Even though he loved tacos, he really craved a hamburger. Finally, a sign appeared for "The Best Burgers in the West." Growing hungrier just reading the sign, Andy pulled in to the parking lot. Happy and relieved at the same time, he grabbed his wallet and went inside.

"I'd like a burger, fries, and a vanilla shake, please."

"Just five minutes, sir." Kicking the counter with his foot, Andy wanted to cry because he was so hungry. Laughing and giggling on the cell phone, the woman ignored poor Andy.

"Ma'am, may I order?"

"Not right now, sir!"

"Okay, but I'm really hungry. Please may I order?"

"Quiet, sir!" Reeling from hunger and anger, Andy left the burger joint. Shame on her, Andy thought. That's the last time I go to the Wacky Wanna Burger! Until I eat dinner I can't drive another mile, he thought. Very grouchy and now starving, Andy couldn't think straight. When all hope seemed to be lost, a few bright neon signs flashed in the distance. "Xerox Copies" was a sign that glowed blue and made Andy blue because he certainly couldn't eat paper, but then he noticed another sign, a sign that glowed red and read "Fast Food Fast." "Yes!" Andy yelled aloud. Zestfully, Andy skipped across the parking lot and to the counter to order some greasy fare that would keep him going for miles.

163.   I wouldn't marry you even if the entire future of civilization depended on us marrying and having children.

I wouldn't marry you even if I had a choice between you and jumping into a vat of lemon juice with paper cuts all over my body.

I wouldn't marry you even if you became the multi-millionaire owner of Ben & Jerry's ice cream and gave me a lifetime supply of Cherry Garcia.

I wouldn't marry you even if you won the lottery and offered to buy me absolutely anything I wanted for the rest of my life.

I wouldn't marry you even if I had no prospect of ever finding another man interested enough in me to propose and I knew I would have to spend the rest of my life alone and raising cats for company.

164. Susie sells seashells since summer's started, sometimes singing songs softly, sifting sand simultaneously. Seagulls swiftly sailing skyward swoop suddenly, so Susie startles. Since seagulls seldom scare Susie, she simply sighs, searching sandy spots, seeking several special shells, so she scarcely sees the seagulls.

165. Milford was happy to be warm and **dry** inside his car. As he put his seatbelt on, he looked out at the driving rain. The road was soaking **wet** just beyond his short driveway. "It's going to be a **slow** morning on the freeway," he said as he started his car and revved the engine. When the engine roared to life, it made a **loud** racket, but then it settled down to a **quiet** purr. He pulled out of the driveway and made his way to the freeway entrance as **fast** as he could. Once on the freeway, Milford found a safe and comfortable position behind a **large** semi truck. The truck was **high** enough to block the sheets of north-driving rain from hitting the windshield of his **small** car. When he reached the **low** valley of suburbs just before the city, he slowed down and began searching for his exit.

166.   I would choose a greyhound for Lance Armstrong because greyhounds are fast.

I would choose a Saint Bernard for Oprah because Saint Bernards like to help people.

I would choose a Husky for Tiger Woods because Huskies are hard-working.

I would choose a border collie for Bill Gates because border collies are smart.

I would choose a bulldog for Arnold Schwarzenegger because bulldogs are tough.

167. No. No, sir. I will not. I will not go. You can't make me go. Maybe you can go by yourself. Hank, please stop asking me to go. I have to work the day you go. It sounds like you will not go without me. If I go, how much would you pay me, Hank?

168. *Grand M* would be an appropriate name for Eldora because she is a sophisticated kind of lady with a grand air about her. GM might work, too. After all, she drives cars by General Motors. She could also be *Miss E.* It has a nice sound, and since the divorce, she isn't a Mrs. anymore. Another good name for Eldora would be *Lady Fishbein* because it sounds

older and sophisticated, but not "grandmotherly." Finally, if she wanted something cuddlier and friendlier, she might try shortening either her first name or her last name to *Eldie* or *Fishy*—though maybe *Fishy* isn't the best idea in the world.

169. I love to eat at Avogadro's Number, a small quirky joint that features live music, including jazz, blues and bluegrass. Avo's has lots of wonderful food, including my favorite, hummus in pita pockets. It's a great place to get your food and music fix, all in one stop.

170.
      I think that I shall never miss
      Another phone call, thanks to this
      Machine that captures every call
      And lets me hear them after all;
      This device is on both night and day
      To capture calls when I'm away;
      It's something I can't do without,
      And if I had it not, I doubt
      I'd ever have another date
      Because I'd be perpetually late.
      Answering machine greetings are made by fools like me,
      Only you can leave a message and fill me with glee.

171. The television show, "What NOT to Believe," will feature young people who are selected based on their gullibility. The roster of naive youngsters will include those who believe that they will be making $50,000 as soon as they are out of college; those who think they don't have to go to college because they're going to be the next pop star or sports star; and those who are positive they will never set curfews for their own children when they have them. During the show, the young people will encounter real-life people who have believed the same things—and found out the truth the hard way.

172. Computer geeks are a growing population of people that the world needs. Although we may call them "geeks," we probably should call them computer "experts" instead. They would probably appreciate the change. After all, "geek" isn't exactly a title of respect, and we *do* respect them. Most of us would be lost without them. Think about that the next time you want a computer expert to fix *your* computer.

173. One cold, frosty morning in the middle of January, the coldest month of the year in the upper peninsula where natives wear triple thick long underwear and tourists wish they'd gone to Mexico instead, a century-old suspension bridge creaked and groaned in the gale force bitter north wind that howled across the frozen bay, before it twisted and broke away from its moorings, plunging with its lone, unknown pedestrian down into the icy, snowy darkness below, which leads us to the question with which we must now struggle, "Who was the lone pedestrian crossing the bridge that cold and frosty morning, and why wasn't he wearing any clothes?"

174. Olivia wants the world to know that she is an artist. She always wears a velvet, patchwork

beret on top of her jet black hair. She wears emerald green eye shadow over just her left eye and violet over the right. She accentuates her cheekbones with glitter lotion and wears two large purple crystal earrings that look like they came straight out of my Aunt Millie's costume jewelry box. She always wears a long black turtleneck over a pair of ragged jeans that she has neatly doodled all over in blue ball point pen. She wears an old pearl necklace around her left ankle. Her fingernails are always painted an icy blue. And, on her feet, she loves to wear an old pair of loafers with buttons in the top slot, instead of pennies.

175. My friend Teresa makes me laugh. She makes everyone laugh. She is a very modern kind of gal, but she will throw in really old-fashioned phrases, like "Boy howdy," and "You're darned tootin'!" Somehow, stuff like that is so funny coming out of her. She is very, very short and often turns down food or drink offers by saying, "No, no. I'll pass. I've heard that stunts your growth." She has facial expressions that I just can't explain, but they can reduce even the most serious person to tears of laughter.

176. Advice to parents, from an experienced kid:
    1. Always allow your kids to pick out their own clothes because they are more up on the trends. You may cause your kid to look like a dork, without meaning to.
    2. Always allow your kids to talk on the phone. Sometimes phone calls can be about very urgent matters.
    3. Always give your kids an allowance, especially when they remember to unload the dishwasher after school without being reminded. Kids need to have money of their own.
    4. Always make sure to get your kids to basketball practice on time. If they're late, they may have to run laps, which isn't fair since it wasn't really their fault they were late in the first place.
    5. Always remember that your kids already feel bad when they mess up. You don't have to yell at them and make them feel worse.
    6. Always let your kid use you for an excuse. Sometimes it's easier for kids to say, "My mom won't let me" than "I don't think I should."
    7. Always respect the different music choices your kids may make. Your kids may not like your music, just like your parents probably didn't like yours.
    8. Always look for good things in your kids, even when they are really screwing up. Nobody is all bad.
    9. Always remember that your kids could be a lot worse than they are. For example, some parents have murderers and drug dealers for children.
    10. Always be patient with your kids. If they already knew how to do everything right, they wouldn't need parents.

177. Woe is me. I got my wisdom teeth out last week and I've been eating mashed potatoes and applesauce for every meal ever since. My jaw hurts constantly; all I can do is sit around and watch television. When my friend came over to check up on me, I couldn't open my

mouth wide enough to yell to her to make sure the cat didn't get out, and sure enough, it ran out. My poor, poor lost kitty was out in the cold all alone. I had to spend the afternoon walking around looking for her, and my jaw hurt something fierce! Finally, I found her, but I was so tired by then that I had to take a long nap when I got back home. When I woke up, there was dried drool down my chin. It was gross. I wonder if my jaw will ever be normal again.

178. Forget what you've learned in science class. The real reason that leaves turn brown in the fall has been kept well-hidden for hundreds of years, but now you can know the truth. A colony of beings called Metarbillatastiks, who live just on the outskirts of the center of the Earth, turn leaves brown in the fall by directing heat from the Earth's core up through tree roots. The heat reaches tree leaves and slowly bakes them until they wilt and fall off. The Metarbillatastiks use the dead leaves as fuel to stoke the heat in the Earth's core. They need to keep the core hot in the winter, or it might freeze. So, in the fall, Metarbillatastiks emerge on the Earth's surface to collect dead leaves in the wee hours of morning when no one else is around. They collect the leaves only in unpopulated areas, so no one will notice and thus start asking questions. The Metarbillatastiks take the dead leaves back to the outskirts of the center of the Earth, where they shovel them into a series of furnaces, leading to the Earth's core. The dead leaves feed the fire and keep the Earth running smoothly through the cold winter months. Fortunately, the fall season provides enough dead leaves to keep the Earth running until the next autumn, when the Metarbillatastiks make their dead-leaf-collection journey again.

179.   Version #1: Next time you go shopping at Food World, get in line #13 and notice the cashier as she checks your groceries. She stands in one spot, slides each item across the price scanner and drops it into a bag. This is her routine, and she repeats it a hundred times a day.

    Version #2: Next time you go shopping at Food World, get in line #13 and notice the cashier as she checks your groceries. *She's the perky petite redhead who hums and dances in place as she slides the items across the price scanner, pops them up into the air (except for eggs), and catches them in her other hand before tossing them into the bags like Michael Jordan shooting hoops.* This is her routine, and she repeats it a hundred times a day.

180. Wearing flip-flops and torn jeans, Rusty Fotel approached his favorite heavy metal band, anxious to ask them a few questions. The guitar player offered Rusty a slice of cantaloupe after autographing a poster. Rusty, their number one fan, asked the lead singer why the band didn't play more often in his hometown of Wichita, Kansas. The singer replied, "It's too late to worry about a tour schedule. All I'm thinking about is my toothbrush, toothpaste and a good night's sleep." The band left Rusty standing alone in the dark parking lot. He switched on his key ring flashlight and made the trek back to his car, questions unanswered.

181.   slushy

sloushy: unkempt in appearance; lacking neatness

slouphy: unable to make up one's mind; wishy-washy

The young boy stomped through slushy puddles on his way to school. When he arrived, his teacher stopped him in the hallway. "Your shoes are a mess, your coat is muddy, and your shirt isn't tucked in," she said. "Why are you so sloushy today?"

"What's it to you?" he asked rudely. He didn't care if he was sent to the principal, who was so slouphy that he could never make up his mind to punish anyone.

182. The last few seconds were suspenseful. The score was tied. Our star basketball player almost scored. Then the other team stole the ball. Luckily, they missed their shot. Then our team had another chance. We could win the game. Our star player had the ball. The last second was intense. He jumped high and slammed the ball, scored, and we won!

183. Bob Langowski is the king of kielbasa. He is known all over the Midwest for his speciality sausage making. As you can imagine, being around so much delicious sausage has made Bob a rather extra large man. The only thing larger than Bob is Bob's appetite. In fact, every Friday night Bob takes his wife Minnie to the Hungry Farmer restaurant out on Highway 50. And, every Friday night, Bob takes on the Enormous Ernie Challenge, which challenges any customer to eat a two-pound steak; three baked potatoes with sour cream, butter and bacon; a bowlful of creamy cole slaw and five pieces of Texas toast. If a customer eats all of this, by himself, he gets the whole thing for free. If he can't eat it all, he has to pay the $30 price. Just one look at Bob Langowski, and you know that he never has to pay for his meal at the Hungry Farmer restaurant.

184. Grandma Dorothy is a neat and orderly person. Her house is always impeccably clean. Every knick-knack in her house sits on a doily.

When she's out and about in town running errands or visiting friends, she always wears a hat and a shawl. "You can never be too dressed up!" she says. When she sees a man wearing a suit, she always comments, "He is quite a snappy dresser."

Grandma Dorothy doesn't like mess or chaos. When her grandchildren come to visit, they are not allowed to go anywhere in her house except for the kitchen. Grandma Dorothy insists that they sit quietly at her kitchen table and color in coloring books.

Grandma Dorothy does like to have fun. Every month she goes to the dance at the senior center. She always wants to dance with Mr. Birmingham, but she refuses to break her rule: "A woman should never ask a man to dance."

185. Sputter, Sputter, Little Car

Sputter, sputter, little car,
I know why you can't go far.
Your tires are bald, your engine's shot,
The miles you've gone add up to a lot.
Sputter, sputter, little car,

I know why you can't go far.

If someone drives you way too fast
They'll end up in a body cast.
Your rear axle's rusty and your brakes are bad,
Your overall condition is terribly sad.
Sputter, sputter, little car,
I know why you can't go far.

I wish you luck on future trips,
But sadly, I'm predicting drips.
Your radiator's leaking, after all.
You really need a mechanic's house call.
Sputter, sputter, little car,
I know why you can't go far.

186. dord: little figure that attaches to the dashboard of a car; the head usually bobbles.

I can't wait until I get my own car, even though it will most likely be my grandpa's old Fiat that only runs half the time. I wish I could be cool like my big cousin Frank. He bought this junky old car, and he has totally fixed it up. He painted it this iridescent color that looks green, but when you move, it looks blue. He hooked it up with these hydraulics that make the car hop. The dashboard is covered in a turquoise carpet with the name "Frank" embroidered in it. A little chihuahua dord sits on top of the dashboard, and its head bobbles like crazy when Frank uses the hydraulics.

187. objurate: to reproach or denounce vehemently
scrivener: a notary
predormition: period of semi-consciousness that precedes actual sleep
scrophularia: a family of plants comprising the snapdragon, foxglove, toadflax, etc.
voluminous: having or marked by great volume

My mom was super mad at me when I brought home my report card with a "D" in English. I could tell she was super mad because when she gets super mad, she uses really big words that no one understands. After she read my report card, she said, "You're in voluminous trouble, young man. But before I objurate you, I have to go to the scrivener. While I'm gone, I want you to water the scrophularia and take out the trash. When I get back, I'm going to enjoy a nap, so be quiet and don't disturb my predormition. After my nap, you're going to get an earful about your performance in English class."

188. Savanna peeked through ice on the windshield of her stalled car and saw the remains of two burned buildings. She saw the bars on the windows of the remaining buildings, all in terrible shape. She saw a fire in a barrel in the vacant lot, with people huddled around it.

She thought, briefly, about crying. She thought, briefly, about how dumb it was to set out without a map and wind up in such an unsafe place, on such an unsafe night.

Quickly, she put aside those thoughts. She had her brains. She had a blanket. She had a whole box of chocolate from the Rocky Mountain Chocolate Factory. She had her cell phone. And she had her burly, weight-lifting brother who wasn't afraid of anything, only a phone call away.

"If anyone gives me trouble, I'll toss them some chocolate," she thought, dialing her brother. "If he knows I'm in danger, he'll be here in five minutes, and I can distract anyone with chocolate for only five minutes." She dialed as she tore open the chocolate. She smiled as good old reliable Tank answered her call.

189. ka-bluie, hah-tue, aw-tyu, eh-hoo, ka-chumpf

Mayor Jones has the worst allergies you can imagine. In springtime, he *hah-tues* all day long from all the pollen in the air. The scent of flowering trees is the worst for him. One whiff brings on a big *ka-bluie*. It doesn't get better for him in summer. Anyone going into his office building hears repeated *aw-tyus* resounding down the corridors. Then in fall, he's bothered by all the dry weeds and mold flying in the air. He *eh-hoos* constantly. When winter finally comes, it's the cold dry air that gets to him. You can tell he's nearby with the sound of a little *ka-chumpf* as he goes about his business.

190. The club soda diet is sweeping the nation as the latest diet craze, but this one really works! When you drink club soda with meals or mix it with food, the fizzing action of the carbonation actually dissolves calories so you can eat more without gaining weight and even actually *lose* weight. Drink club soda with potato chips or French fries and cut your calories in half. Use it in recipes in place of liquids like milk or oil and you cut calories by at least one-half—or up to two-thirds if the recipe is a cooked or baked item. The heating of the ingredients in cooked or baked recipes enhances the calorie-destroying action of the added carbonation, making the food even less fattening. This is the best and healthiest diet. It costs almost nothing. You don't have to be hungry, ever, and IT REALLY WORKS!

191. Willard the Wizard was an irrational environmentalist who thought he could solve all the world's environmental problems in the wackiest ways. First he waved his wand and turned every car on Earth into a flower. Then he became worried. Would there be enough bees on the planet to pollinate all of the new flowers he had created? In an instant, however, he came up with a solution: He decided to turn people into bees so that they could pollinate the cars-turned-flowers.

As Willard mulled over his plan, a young girl named Bea was on her way to school. She was skipping along, excited to get to school so she could show her teacher the wonderful job she had done on her assignment. The other kids made fun of her for being a teacher's pet, but Bea didn't care. She was going to go to law school someday.

Suddenly, a wave of blue and orange light passed in front of Bea's eyes. Her backpack dropped to the ground, along with her shoes and clothes. Bea felt strange. She heard a buzzing noise she couldn't escape.

She realized that she had an overpowering urge to become something else—a bee.

"What is happening to me?" she wondered. *Bea had never before wanted to be a bee.*

And then, after another wave of light passed in front of her, she realized the unthinkable. She *was* a bee! It took her a moment to adjust, but soon she was just fine with her new state of bee-ing. As she admired her giant stinger, she decided to go track down those kids in her class who always chided her for being a teacher's pet.

192. There it sits in the YMCA parking lot—an extra large van with navy blue stripes wrapping around it. One peek in the window reveals two car seats, snot-smeared windows, empty juice boxes and melted crayons in the cup holder. The passenger's seat is covered with a week's worth of school projects, including a collage made out of Fruit Loops. Some of the Fruit Loops have been nibbled off. A soccer ball, two tennis rackets and two pairs of arm floaties are on the floor.

      The driver of this car is inside the YMCA teaching an aerobics class. The class is the only thing that keeps Tiffani from looking like the mother of five children, from a seven-year-old down to two-year-old twins. She is still in good shape, despite the thousands of fat-laden grilled cheese sandwiches she has had to scarf down with the children, along with the special grape Kool-Aid that she makes with only half of the sugar.

193. Just as Jar Jar was about to join Queen Amidala's mission, an important call came in from King Gilpora of the planet Zelfore.

      "We need you to assist us with our undercover operation, tentatively titled, "Annoy the Enemy Until They Agree to Surrender."

      "I'm your Gungan!" he said, jumping aboard a special flight, never to be seen again.

194. Arnold's approach to landscape design is truly unique. He has a real passion for lawn ornaments and certainly uses them freely. He especially loves ceramic pigs, painted a very eye-catching shade of purple. Currently, he has 73 of them, in various sizes.

      He also prefers to keep the Christmas spirit alive all year round with his ambitious light displays that cover every inch of his house, as well as all the trees, shrubbery, and lawn ornaments—including the pigs.

      Arnold believes in keeping his neighbors informed. He always tells them, via a bullhorn, when he is going to his mailbox to check his mail. He notifies them, with polite notes taped on their doors, whenever he believes they have done anything to annoy his ceramic pigs, which seem to take offense rather easily.

195. George Weasel approached the woman who was looking over the cars at his dealership.

      "I'll bet you want something sporty," he winked, giving her an appreciative once-over.

      "No," said Fiona Blunt. "I want something practical."

      "Well, practical is okay, but you really look like someone who needs something a little more upscale. Maybe something blue to match those gorgeous eyes of yours."

      "I was thinking of a mini-van."

      "You don't belong in a mini-van! You're much too sophisticated for that. How about this hot little convertible?"

      "How about you telling me where you expect my four kids to ride in something like that? And how you expect me to buy **anything** from someone with your lame lines?" She turned and walked out of the dealership.

196. "Why don't you learn how to talk to a rooster?" Cindy yelled. Her brother was clearly no help in coaxing the rooster into the cage. How were they ever going to get her precious Doodle-Doo to the vet? His comb was looking pale, and he had stopped crowing every morning at 4:30. Sometimes he was as late as 8:00 a.m., and even then the crowing was pretty feeble. He was a sensitive rooster, and one that needed to be handled gently. As she held the cage door open again, her brother bellowed, "Come here, you stupid rooster." That was it. Cindy had had enough of her brother's rough ways. She slugged him.

197. Pat is a 14-year-old boy who lives with his mom and dad. Pat likes videogames, so he was recently disappointed that he didn't receive the game Killer Commandos for his birthday. His parents told him it was too violent, and that they were worried it might adversely affect him. He was pretty darned sure they were wrong. He was also pretty darned unhappy.

Pat tends to sulk when he's unhappy. He mumbles and mopes and slams doors. He's rude to his sister. (Actually, he's rude to his sister even when he isn't unhappy.) His parents roll their eyes and try to ignore him, unless he becomes too obnoxious. Then they send him to his room, just so they don't have to deal with him.

Last Sunday afternoon, Pat visited his grandmother, as usual, and she made him very, very happy. She gave him a special birthday present—$50.00. With what he had already saved, he knew he had enough to buy Killer Commandos. When he got home, he told his parents he was going to ride his bike to the mall.

Unfortunately for Pat, his sister spoke up. "I see you have an envelope from Grandma. How much money did you get?"

"None of your business," said Pat.

"I'll bet it's enough to get you interested in riding your bike to the mall. What are you going to buy?"

"None of your business," said Pat.

"It isn't Killer Commandos, is it?" said his sister.

"None of your business," said Pat.

His parents finally tuned in to the conversation. "Pat, if buying Killer Commandos is your intention, you'd better get that out of your head. You're not allowed to have Killer Commandos, and that's final."

"I can't believe this!" yelled Pat. "This is so lame! What right do you have to tell me what to do?"

His parents looked at him and sighed. "We're your parents," his father said. "Live with it."

Pat stomped upstairs.

"Does this mean you're not going to the mall now?" his sister called, ever so sweetly.

198. I'll bet he could lift a truck if he wanted to!
Look at that six-pack!

I'll bet he runs marathons.

He should be a professional bodyguard.

All he needs is a handle-bar mustache and he could join the circus as a strong man.

You wouldn't want him as an opponent in an arm wrestling competition.

199.   Rock-a-Bye-Baby.

Safe in my arms.

I will protect you,

keep you from harm.

I hold you tightly,

next to my heart.

Nothing will ever

tear us apart.

200. The Applewood Estates Homeowners' Association has the personality of a fussbudgety old maid in a movie from the 1950s. The group has its nose in everything. Want to paint your fence white? It has to decide if you have chosen the right white for the neighborhood. In its opinion (and it is never wrong!), all homeowners should choose White Effervescence, never Eggshell or Snow Symphony. If you should forget to get the Association's approval, well, you will have to pay the consequences. Rules are rules. You will have to repaint, unless, by chance, you have chosen White Effervescence.

About the Authors

Dawn DiPrince teaches specialty writing classes to elementary and middle school students and memoir writing classes to senior adults. She is the founder of *BlueSky Quarterly*, a magazine that celebrates life in southeastern Colorado. She lives in Pueblo, Colorado, with her husband and three young children.

Cheryl Miller Thurston taught English and writing classes for more than 13 years, grades seven through university level. She is the author of many plays, musicals, and books for teachers. She lives with her husband and two pampered cats in Loveland, Colorado.

Common Core State Standards Alignment

Grade Level	Common Core State Standards
Grade 7 ELA-Literacy	W.7.3 Write narratives to develop real or imagined experiences or events using effective technique, relevant descriptive details, and well-structured event sequences.
	W.7.5 With some guidance and support from peers and adults, develop and strengthen writing as needed by planning, revising, editing, rewriting, or trying a new approach, focusing on how well purpose and audience have been addressed. (Editing for conventions should demonstrate command of Language standards 1–3 up to and including grade 7 here.)
	W.7.10 Write routinely over extended time frames (time for research, reflection, and revision) and shorter time frames (a single sitting or a day or two) for a range of discipline-specific tasks, purposes, and audiences.
	L.7.3 Use knowledge of language and its conventions when writing, speaking, reading, or listening.
	L.7.5 Demonstrate understanding of figurative language, word relationships, and nuances in word meanings.
Grade 8 ELA-Literacy	W.8.3 Write narratives to develop real or imagined experiences or events using effective technique, relevant descriptive details, and well-structured event sequences.
	W.8.5 With some guidance and support from peers and adults, develop and strengthen writing as needed by planning, revising, editing, rewriting, or trying a new approach, focusing on how well purpose and audience have been addressed. (Editing for conventions should demonstrate command of Language standards 1–3 up to and including grade 8 here.)
	W.8.10 Write routinely over extended time frames (time for research, reflection, and revision) and shorter time frames (a single sitting or a day or two) for a range of discipline-specific tasks, purposes, and audiences.
	L.8.1 Demonstrate command of the conventions of standard English grammar and usage when writing or speaking.
	L.8.5 Demonstrate understanding of figurative language, word relationships, and nuances in word meanings.
Grade 9–10 ELA-Literacy	W.9-10.3 Write narratives to develop real or imagined experiences or events using effective technique, well-chosen details, and well-structured event sequences.
	W.9-10.5 Develop and strengthen writing as needed by planning, revising, editing, rewriting, or trying a new approach, focusing on addressing what is most significant for a specific purpose and audience. (Editing for conventions should demonstrate command of Language standards 1–3 up to and including grades 9–10 here.)

Grade Level	Common Core State Standards
Grade 9–10 ELA-Literacy, *continued*	W.9-10.10 Write routinely over extended time frames (time for research, reflection, and revision) and shorter time frames (a single sitting or a day or two) for a range of tasks, purposes, and audiences.
	L.9-10.1 Demonstrate command of the conventions of standard English grammar and usage when writing or speaking.
	L.9-10.5 Demonstrate understanding of figurative language, word relationships, and nuances in word meanings.
Grade 11–12 ELA-Literacy	W.11-12.3 Write narratives to develop real or imagined experiences or events using effective technique, well-chosen details, and well-structured event sequences.
	W.11-12.5 Develop and strengthen writing as needed by planning, revising, editing, rewriting, or trying a new approach, focusing on addressing what is most significant for a specific purpose and audience. (Editing for conventions should demonstrate command of Language standards 1–3 up to and including grades 11–12 here.).
	W.11-12.10 Write routinely over extended time frames (time for research, reflection, and revision) and shorter time frames (a single sitting or a day or two) for a range of tasks, purposes, and audiences.
	L.11-12.5 Demonstrate understanding of figurative language, word relationships, and nuances in word meanings.